商务英语入门

Introduction to Business English

主　编　陈惠惠　田　杰　刘玉君
编　者　华　捷　裘莹莹　林春洋
　　　　刘海燕　李赛男

图书在版编目(CIP)数据

商务英语入门/陈惠惠,田杰,刘玉君主编. —北京：北京大学出版社，2015.10
（大学英语立体化网络化系列教材·拓展课程教材）
ISBN 978-7-301-26323-5

Ⅰ.①商⋯　Ⅱ.①陈⋯②田⋯③刘⋯　Ⅲ.①商务 – 英语 – 高等学校 – 教材　Ⅳ.①H31

中国版本图书馆 CIP 数据核字（2015）第 225371 号

书　　　名	商务英语入门 SHANGWU YINGYU RUMEN
著作责任者	陈惠惠　田 杰　刘玉君　主编
责 任 编 辑	郝妮娜
标 准 书 号	ISBN 978-7-301-26323-5
出 版 发 行	北京大学出版社
地　　　址	北京市海淀区成府路 205 号　100871
网　　　址	http://www.pup.cn　新浪微博:@北京大学出版社
电 子 信 箱	zbing@pup.pku.edu.cn
电　　　话	邮购部 62752015　发行部 62750672　编辑部 62759634
印 刷 者	北京鑫海金澳胶印有限公司
经 销 者	新华书店
	730 毫米 × 980 毫米　16 开本　6.75 印张　200 千字 2015 年 10 月第 1 版　2022 年 2 月第 5 次印刷
定　　　价	28.00 元

未经许可，不得以任何方式复制或抄袭本书之部分或全部内容。
版权所有，侵权必究
举报电话: 010-62752024　电子信箱: fd@pup.pku.edu.cn
图书如有印装质量问题，请与出版部联系，电话: 010-62756370

前　言

近年来，世界经济一体化的迅猛发展使得中外合资、外商独资等外向型企业不断涌入内地市场，随着地方企业对外交流需求日益增多，企业对具有较强的英语交际及实际应用能力的卓越外语人才需求极为迫切。越来越多的大学生希望涉足商务英语，以期能够在未来的社会竞争中更好地抓住机遇，迎接挑战，适应社会对优秀英语复合型人才的需求。同时，《国家中长期人才发展规划纲要（2010—2020年）》中明确指出，高等工程教育应需强化主动服务国家战略需求、主动服务行业企业需求的意识，竭力培养一大批能够适应和支撑产业发展、具有创新能力及国际竞争力的工程人才。

《商务英语入门》是高等学校英语拓展系列教程中大学英语后续课程，主要介绍商务英语礼仪与实践的相关知识，通过提供一些英语国家的文化背景知识、现代电子商务知识和面试、谈判事务、商务广告等，帮助学生提高语言的实际应用能力。

《商务英语入门》为商务英语的入门教材，主要内容为：商务英语内涵及意义，现代商务英语礼仪，商务英语广告，商务英语实践，商务英语会话，商务英语谈判及商务求职面试。通过本课程的学习，旨在培养学生掌握商务英语礼仪与实践的相关知识，了解现代商务英语的特点，提高商务英语实践方面的能力，帮助对商务英语感兴趣的学生积累基础知识，以便后续自学，以达到通识教育的目的。

本书具有以下特色：

• 内容章节丰富，实用性强。涵盖商务礼仪、商务广告、商务会话、谈判及求职。深入浅出地介绍商务领域的基础知识与理论，帮助学生了解实用商务知识，熟悉商务英语表达。提高学生对教材内容的兴趣，易于授课教师调动课堂气氛。

• 结构清晰明了，简明性强。每个章节包括章节目标、导入、课文A、课文B、案例分析、补充材料、注释、课后练习等等。方便学生查找课文内容及注释，帮助学生理解教材内容。

• 文字阐述配有表格、图片等，直观、清晰地呈现商务知识，帮助学生更好地运用形象思维理清知识结构。

• 设有"案例分析"板块，并配有讨论题。通过阅读和分析真实的商业案例，进一步提高学生运用知识的能力，提高他们分析问题、解决问题的能力，增强他们对商业社会的了解。

本书共有六章，分别为商务英语概述、商务英语礼仪、商务英语广告、商务英语会话、商务英语谈判、求职就业六章。具体内容为：

• 商务英语概述：简单介绍Business，Business English，Commercial English内涵及特点。

• 商务英语礼仪：着重介绍商务场合得体的着装、待人接物及会话礼仪。

• 商务英语广告：着重介绍商务广告的特点、优秀的广告创意及其简练的英语表达。

• 商务英语会话：简单介绍商务会话的原则及商务场合正式的会话礼貌用语和会话技巧。

• 商务英语谈判：简单介绍商务谈判的原则及案例分析。

• 商务求职面试：着重介绍求职信、履历表的规范性及面试过程中需要注意的重要事项。

本书适合普通高等院校二、三、四年级本科学生使用，主要作为非英语专业学生达到四级水平以后的后续选修课程教材使用。建议授课教师两到三周讲授一个单元，着重讲授商务英语礼仪、广告及求职面试章节。希望教师以讲授商务理论、教授学生实践知识为主，辅助学习正式的商务表达。

全书由陈惠惠老师总体设计，田杰、刘玉君老师协助规范选材、格式等，编写凝聚了淮阴工学院商务英语课题组成员的共同努力。在编写校稿过程中得到了北京大学出版社黄瑞明编辑、郝妮娜编辑的大力支持，她们提出了许多中肯的修改意见，使得本书进一步完善和规范。在此，一并致谢。

编者

2015年9月

Contents

Unit One Brief Introduction to Business English ·· 1
    Text A Business and Business English ·· 1
    Text B Characteristics of Business English ·· 3

Unit Two Business Etiquette ·· 16
    Text A Business Etiquette ·· 16
    Text B Table Manners and Culture Differences ·· 20
    Text C Dress for Business Success ·· 25

Unit Three Business Advertising ·· 34
    Text A Introduction to Advertising ·· 35
    Text B Characteristics of Advertising Language ·· 39

Unit Four Business English Conversation ·· 52
    Text A Business English Conversation Theory ·· 52
    Text B Active Listening Keeps Conversation Going ·· 55

Unit Five Business Negotiation ·· 68
    Text A Business Negotiation ·· 68
    Text B Basic Rules of Business Negotiation ·· 70

Unit Six Job Interview ·· 84
    Text A Introduction to Job Application Letter ·· 84
    Text B How to Write a Resume? ·· 87

Brief Introduction to Business English

Unit One

Objectives

To understand and appreciate the significance of business and business English.
To learn some theme-related words, expressions and sentences.
To learn the formal business expression through 7Cs principles.
To discuss and present ideas about business English.

Lead in

1. What activities do you think can be labeled as business activities? Have you ever been involved in any business activities before? If yes, please share your experiences with us.
2. What do you think is important for success in today's business world?

Text A

Business and Business English

Business

   Business is the human activity related to material things. It is necessary for civilization. It is found in all societies, even the simplest ones. Business may include the production of goods: Making airplanes, building buildings and constructing paper boxes are examples of production. It can also provide the financing for these activities. Lending money, trading stocks and bonds, and selling insurance policies relate to the securing of capital for business activities. Other forms of business include merchandising, which is the selling of products, and providing various services, such as accounting, distributing and repairs. Business, then, is the activity of producing and distributing goods and services.

Commerce is the exchange of items of value between persons or companies. Any exchange of money for a product, service, or information is considered as a deal of commerce. Commerce has been a constant part of history.

E-commerce (electronic commerce), is online commerce versus real-world commerce. E-commerce includes retail shopping, banking, stocks and bonds trading, auctions, real estate transactions, airline booking, movie rentals—nearly anything you can imagine in the real world. Even personal services such as hair and nail salons can benefit from e-commerce by providing a website for the sale of related health and beauty products, normally available to local customers exclusively.

Business English

Business English is the English language especially related to international trade. It is a part of English for Specific Purposes and can be considered as a specialty within English language learning and teaching. Much of the English communication that takes place within business circles all over the world occurs between non-native speakers. In such cases, the object of the exercise is efficient and effective communication. The strict rules of grammar are in such cases sometimes ignored, when, for example, a stressed negotiator's only goal is to reach an agreement as quickly as possible.

Business English means different things to different people. For some, it focuses on vocabulary and topics used in the worlds of business, trade, finance, and international relations. For others it refers to the communication skills used in the workplace, and focuses on the language and skills needed for typical business communication such as presentations, negotiations, meetings, small talk, socializing, correspondence, report writing, and so on.

The Differences Between Business English and General English

In a broad sense, the content is different since the topics of business English will be related to the workplace or world of business. So instead of family and friends, a business English course book may contain topics like global business cultures, or a day in the life at the office. The skills may be business communication skills like delivering presentations rather than speaking in general. With the new titles like "Natural English" and "Skills for life", the focus is changing as English's role as the lingua franca to new heights. The demand for business English is now more than ever an instrumental demand for general English.

In today's global economy, learners not only want the skills to read, write, listen to and speak English fluently, they also want to be able to communicate in a way which will be recognized and appreciated by their counterparts in the international arena. Instead of pair work and group work, students of business English will learn more through case studies, role play and simulation exercises. You are more likely to be a facilitator when learning meeting skills or a mediator when learning monitoring a negotiation.

Text B

Characteristics of Business English

Nick Brieger, professor of business English, believes that business English should include language knowledge, communication skills, professional content, management skills and cultural awareness, etc. Since it is one of the branches of English language and serves as ESP (English for Specific Purpose), business English has the common traits of common English as well as its unique characteristics in its vocabulary, formality, concrete language and concise sentences.

In business English, we have 7Cs principles as Completeness, Correctness, Conciseness, Clearness, Concreteness, Courtesy and Consideration. For example, this corporation is specialized in handling the import and export business in electronic products and wishes to enter into business relations with you.

1. **Completeness:** Keep in mind the following guidelines to write completely.

    1) Try to answer all questions asked.

    Whenever you reply to a letter containing one or more questions, try to answer all of them stated or implied. If you have no information on a precise question at the moment, just say so clearly and sincerely, instead of leaving out the answer. If you have unfavorable news in answer to one or more questions, handle your reply with both tact and honesty. When your answer is no, be courteous and polite but firm.

    2) Add something that may be of some use to your reader now or in the future.

    3) Check for the 5W2H and any other essentials.

    5W2H: Who, What, Where, When, Why, How, How much.

    In a letter of ordering goods, we must tell clearly about What (What we want), When (When we need the goods), Whom and Where (to Whom and Where the goods to be sent), How (How payment will be made, How we would like them to be packed and shipped), How much (How much goods we need). For some letters, especially those that bring bad news, answering the question "why" is of vital importance.

2. **Conciseness:** Express ideas in the fewest words without sacrificing completeness and courtesy.

    1) Omit trite expressions.

    2) Avoid wordy statements and unnecessary repetition.

    3) Remove all the irrelevant facts in your message.

Major causes of irrelevancy mainly include: not coming to the point, including information obvious to the reader, using big words to make an impression, being excessive polite, making too many unnecessary explanation, not revising the first draft of a long, complicated message.

3. **Consideration:** Keep in mind to consider and maximize benefit to others.

   1) Use "you" attitude instead of "we" attitude.

   2) Be aware of some notable exceptions where "you" attitude is not suitable.

4. **Concreteness:** Be specific, definite, and vivid rather than vague and general.

   1) Use specific facts and figures.

   2) Use verbs of action: Put action in verbs instead of nouns or infinitives.

5. **Clearness:** Keep writing clearly.

   1) Avoid using words or structures that cause ambiguity.

   2) Be careful of the position of the attributives.

   3) Be attentive to the position of nouns and prons.

6. **Courtesy:** Give the receiver a feeling of importance and satisfaction.

   1) Answer your mail immediately.

   2) Be sincere and naturally tactful, thoughtful and appreciative.

   3) Avoid using expressions that may irritate your reader.

7. **Correctness:** Choose the correct level of language, have a good command of both Chinese and English, and use only accurate facts, figures and words.

   1) Choose the correct level of language.

   A. Formal: Top-level government documents and papers, dissertations and theses, international agreements, legal documents and other institutional writings.

   B. Informal: Business letters, newspaper and magazine articles, publication for general use, and letters exchanged between friends and relatives.

   2) Have a good command of English. Figures and numbers should be correct.

   From the above 7Cs principles, we can see that the final deal is the ultimate goal of writing business letters with clear, concise language and in a complete, correct and polite way to express the intention of the writer. In the writing process, we should not only ensure correct spelling, grammar, syntax, but also pay attention to sentence structure, choice of words and consider the reader's feelings.

7Cs correspondence principle as an important method of writing instruction can not only help writers write letters from the proposed specific standards of quality, but also further the writer's attitude and state of mind to put forward higher requirements.

Case Study

Case One:

Distinguish which expression is better according to the above mentioned 7Cs principles.

1) We cannot deliver the goods until May 1.

   We can deliver the goods on May 1.

2) We regret to inform you that we deny your request for credit.

   For the time being we can only serve you on a cash basis.

3) I am writing to you at this time to enclose in this letter a tentative plan for the forthcoming visit to California by our Director Mr. Neil next August when we might get together to discuss matters of mutual interest.

   Here is a tentative plan for Mr. Neil's visit to California next August.

4) We hereby wish to let you know that we fully appreciate the confidence you have reposed in our products.

   We appreciate your confidence in our products.

5) We would like to know whether you would allow us to extend the time of shipment for twenty days, and if you would be as kind as to allow us to do so, kindly give us your reply by cable without delay.

   Please reply by cable immediately if you will allow us to delay the shipment until April 21.

6) We are happy to have your order for Gentlemen shirts, which we are sending today by CAAC Flight No. 345.

   Your selection of Gentlemen shirts should reach you by Saturday, as they were shipped today by CAAC Flight No. 345.

7) You failed to enclose your pamphlet in the envelope.

The envelope we received did not have your pamphlet in it.
8) We will give a favorable consideration to your suggestions.
   We will consider your suggestions favorably.
9) As instructed, we should send to your branch office in Shanghai 2 barrels of Turpentine Oil containing 25 gallons.
   As instructed, we shall send to your branch office in Shanghai two barrels of Turpentine Oil each containing 25 gallons or containing 25 gallons each.
10) We are sending you in the enclosed list five samples of the goods for your market which we think suitable by air freight.
    As in the enclosed list, we are sending you by air freight five samples of the goods which we think suitable for your market.

Case Two:

1) Omit trite expressions

Not This	But This
Please don't hesitate to write to us	Please write us
due to the fact that	because
during the year of 2003	during 2003
in the city of London	London
in due course	soon
for the reason that	since; because
in the event that	if
this is to advise you	advise
from the point of view of	as
for a price of $200,000	for $200,000
in accordance with your request	as you requested; as requested

2) Choose the correct level of language

Formal	Informal
anticipate	expect
ascertain	find out
deem	think (believe)

terminate	end
endeavor	try
interrogate	ask
procure	get
utilize	use

3) Figures and numbers should be correct

A. $2 or (and) above (over)	60 dozen or (and) up (upwards)
$2 or (and) less (below)	60 dozen or (and) down (downwards)
2% or (and) more	
an order for 50 gross or upward	an order for not less than 50 gross
B. 5% up to 10% both inclusive	over 5% up to 10% inclusive
any excess over 3%	any amount over and above 3%
a sum exceeding 3%	a sum above 3%

Case Three:

1) Try to answer all questions asked in the ordering letter.

Dear Sir or Madam,

    Many thanks for your order of October 12.

    After careful consideration, we have come to the conclusion that it would be better for you to approach another manufacturer for the products you desire. To produce the machine required according to your specifications would mean setting up special equipment at our factory. This would not only be impossible to accomplish before the end of this year, but would seriously interrupt our production schedule.

    We are sorry not to be more helpful, but hope that you will understand our position. Please contact us again. We will be pleased to serve you in the future.

Yours sincerely,
Rocky

2) Try to appreciate the careful choices of formal business words and phrases.

Dear Sirs,

    It is reported in a domestic newspaper that the Iranian Central Bank has

Unit One Brief Introduction to Business English

instructed the commercial banks to suspend their business of opening a new letter of credit as from the 3rd May for financial reason of foreign currency. Although it is said that this arrangement would be a temporary one and with establishment of new import policy this emergency arrangement would be lifted, we are much concerned about the outcome of this movement toward restriction of import to Iran and shall be obliged if you will kindly keep us well advised of development of this new arrangement especially in connection with import from France.

Yours sincerely,
David

Notes

1. **People or Organizations Engaged in Business**
   company, firm, enterprise, joint-venture, corporation, individual company, collective factory, private company, conglomerate, manager, merchant, salesman, businessman

2. **Places to Conduct Business Activities**
   market, department store, supermarket, stock exchange, hotel, restaurant, bank

3. **Other Terms Frequently Used in Business Operation**
   sell, buy, goods, order, profit, interest, invoice, check, bill, consumer, customer

4. **Professional Terms and Abbreviation**
   Insurance: Free from Particular Average, With Particular Average, All Risks
   Terms of price: FOB (free on board), CIF (cost, insurance and freight), CFR (cost and freight)
   Terms of payment: M/T (mail transfer), T/T (telegraphic transfer), D/D (demand draft), D/P (documents against payment), D/A (documents against acceptance), L/C (letter of credit)

5. **Formality**
   concur / come together, terminate or expiry / end, prior to or previous to / before, in view of / because of, certify / prove, in the nature of / like, along the lines of / like, for the purpose of / for, in the case of / if, on the ground that / since/because, with reference to or with regard to / about, etc.

Useful Words

1. appointment 约会，约定
2. assignment 分配；工作
3. colleague 同事，同僚
4. receptionist 接待员
5. buyout/buy out 买进全部产权或股权；收购全部
6. equity 公平；公正；扣除抵押、税金后的剩余财产价值
7. financier 财政家；金融业者；资本家；投资者
8. franchise 经销权；加盟权
9. prospectus 计划书；说明书；募股书
10. subsidiary 子公司

Useful Expressions

1. I've heard so much about you.
2. You've had a long day. You've had a long flight.
3. Distinguished / Honorable / Respected friends / Your Excellency: On behalf of the Beijing Municipal government, I wish to extend our warm welcome to the friends who have come to visit Beijing.
4. On behalf of the Beijing Municipal government, I wish to express our heartfelt thanks to you for your gracious assistance.
5. American businessmen are welcome to make investment in Beijing.
6. Your valuable advice is most welcome.
7. It's a rewarding trip!
8. As you have a tight schedule, I will not take up more of your time.
9. Thank you so much for coming. Please remember me to Mr. Wang.
10. If you want to be your own boss, you will probably encounter some rough patches along the road to the big rewards.

Supplementary Materials

Practical Wisdom: The Right Way to Do the Right Thing
Barry Schwartz

We Americans are growing increasingly disenchanted with the institutions on which we depend. We can't trust them. They disappoint us. They fail to give us what we need. This is true of schools that are not serving our kids as well as we think they should. It is true of doctors who seem too busy to give us the attention and unhurried care we crave. It's true of banks that mismanage our assets, and of bond-rating agencies that fail to provide an accurate assessment of the risk of possible investments. It's true of a legal system that seems more interested in expedience than in justice. It's true of a workplace in which we fulfill quotas and hit targets and manage systems but wind up feeling disconnected from the animating forces that drew us to our careers in the first place. And the disenchantment we experience as recipients of services is often matched by the dissatisfaction of those who provide them.

Most doctors want to practice medicine well and keep up with the latest medical research, but they feel helpless faced with the challenge of balancing patients' needs with the practical demands of hassling with insurance companies, earning enough to pay malpractice premiums and squeezing patients into seven-minute visits. Most teachers want to teach kids the basics and at the same time instill a passion for learning, but they feel helpless faced with the challenge of reconciling these goals with mandates to meet targets on standardized tests, to adopt specific teaching techniques and to keep up with the ever-increasing paperwork. No one is satisfied—not the professionals and not their clients.

When we try to make things better, we generally reach for one of two tools. The first tool is a set of rules and procedures that tell people what to do and monitor their performance. The second tool is a set of incentives that encourage good performance by rewarding people for it. The assumption behind carefully constructed rules is that even if people do want to do the right thing, they need to be told what that is. And the assumption underlying incentives is that people will not be motivated to do the right thing unless they have an incentive to do so. Rules and incentives. Sticks and carrots. What else is there?

Our new book, *Practical Wisdom: The Right Way to Do the Right Thing* is an attempt to answer that question. Rules and incentives are not enough. They leave out something essential—what classical philosopher Aristotle called practical wisdom (his word was phronesis). Without this missing ingredient, neither detailed rules nor clever incentives will be enough to solve the problems we face.

Most experienced practitioners know that rules only take them so far. How should a doctor balance respect for patient choice with the knowledge that sometimes the patient is not the best judge of what is needed? How should a doctor balance the need to spend enough time with each patient to be thorough, compassionate and understanding with the need to see enough patients to keep the office solvent? How should a doctor balance the desire to tell patients the truth, no matter how difficult, with the desire to be kind?

Doctors—and teachers attempting to teach and inspire, or lawyers attempting to provide proper counsel and serve justice—are not puzzling over a choice between the "right" thing and the "wrong" thing. The common quandaries they face are choices among right things—right things that clash. A good doctor needs to be honest with her patients, and kind to her patients, and give them the hope they need to endure difficult treatments. But, these aims are often at odds, and the doctor must decide whether to be honest or compassionate, or more likely how to balance honesty and compassion in a way that is appropriate for the patient in front of her.

Aristotle recognized that balancing acts like these beg for wisdom, and that wisdom has to be practical because the conundrums we face are embedded in our everyday work. They are quandaries that any practitioner must resolve to do her work well. Practical wisdom combines the will to do the right thing with the skill to figure out what the right thing is.

Our book describes the essential characteristics of practical wisdom and shows why it's needed to inform the everyday activities of doctors, lawyers, teachers and parents, lovers and friends. We discuss some impressive examples of wisdom and its absence in practice. We show that the rules and incentives we reach for to improve our schools or our clinics or even our banks are no substitute for wisdom. Worse, they can be the enemies of wise practice. We examine best practices that actually encourage the development of wisdom. And finally, we suggest that when wisdom is cultivated it is not only good for society but is, as Aristotle thought, a key to our own happiness. Wisdom isn't just something we "ought" to have. It's something we want to have to flourish.

In our efforts to make things better, we rely on two tools—detailed rules and smart incentives. But neither of these tools is up to the task. Rules subvert people's ability to find novel solutions to novel problems. And incentives only encourage people to go through life asking "what's in it for me?" instead of "what can I do to help?" What we need, beyond rules and incentives, is character—virtue. And the particular virtue we need above all is what Aristotle called "practical wisdom".

A wise person knows when to follow rules and when to improvise around them.

A wise person can take the perspective of the people she serves, and empathize with them.

A wise person can improvise.

And a wise person uses these skills in the service of the right aims.

Questions:

1. *What does classical philosopher Aristotle mean phronesis?*
2. *What does the phrase practical wisdom mean by Barry Schwartz? And what is practical wisdom in your mind?*
3. *Which one is of the most significance in business success in your opinion?*

Assignments

1. Translate the following paragraph about the definition of business into Chinese.

Business is the human activity related to material things. It is necessary for civilization. It is found in all societies, even the simplest ones. Business may include the production of goods: Making airplanes, building buildings and constructing paper boxes are examples of production. It can also provide the financing for these activities. Lending money, trading stocks and bonds, and selling insurance policies relate to the securing of capital for business activities. Other forms of business include merchandising, which is the selling of products, and providing various services, such as accounting, distributing and repairs. Business, then, is the activity of producing and distributing goods and services.

2. Appreciate the following sentences and try to find the more formal expression.

1) a. They informed Messrs. John & Smith that they would receive an answer in a few days.

   b. They informed Messrs. John & Smith that the latter would receive an answer in a few days.

2) a. We are willing to leave this matter to the company the details of which are unknown to us.

   b. We are willing to leave the company this matter, the details of which are unknown to us.

3) a. The goods we received contrary to our instructions are packed in wooden cases without iron hoops.

   b. The goods we received are packed in wooden cases without iron hoops contrary to our instructions.

4) a. We shall be able to supply 10 cases of the item only.

   b. We shall be able to supply only 10 cases of the item.

5) a. You are entirely wrong in your attitude concerning our claim.

   b. We'd like to explain in more detail why you are responsible for the loss of our ordered goods.

3. What does business English refer to you? What do you want to learn from our business English course? Think about which part is of your favorite interest. Give your reason.
4. What are the essential elements for business success in your mind?
5. Being a successful businessman or businesswoman, what kind of virtues should you own?

Unit Two

Business Etiquette

Objectives

To understand and appreciate the significance of business etiquette.
To learn some theme-related words, expressions, and sentences of business etiquette.
To learn some table manners and dress etiquette for business success.
To discuss and present ideas about business etiquette.

Lead in

1. What is the proper time to arrive for an appointment? Can you exchange business cards while dining?
2. What will you dress for a job interview to make a good impression?
3. How can you get more privacy in your cubicle without being rude to your coworkers?

Text A

Business Etiquette

Etiquette is a set of rules that allow us to interact with others in a civilized manner, such as treating other people with courtesy and respect and making them feel comfortable with you. Maybe you are always polite and courteous to others, but there are differences between Chinese and western etiquette, for example, asking someone's age is offensive to an American.

Unit Two Business Etiquette

Business etiquette is not just knowing what to discuss during a business dinner or how to address colleagues; it is a way of presenting yourself in such a way that you will be taken seriously. This involves demonstrating that you have the self-control necessary to be good at your job, expressing knowledge of business situations and having the ability to make others comfortable around you. Poor business etiquette can cost you the trust of your coworkers and your customers, and the loss of valuable business opportunities.

1. Courtesy

One of the most basic elements of business etiquette is courtesy, or respect, which should be displayed to the people you work with, including your customers, no matter what. You should consider the feelings of others and address conflicts in a straightforward and impersonal manner. Raising your voice, using bad language and interrupting others is discourteous and shows disrespect for others. People who are disrespectful may find themselves losing credibility and the respect of their peers.

2. Building Relationship

Show others that you value their work by taking time to visit and talk with them. This can include not only your immediate colleagues, but also people who work under you, such as secretaries and janitorial staff. These people can help you look more professional and will go the extra mile for you if you treat them with respect. Make time to actually talk to people; do not rush off immediately after exchanging greetings. You can also create a database of your colleagues and contacts, in which you list their birthdays, spouses' names and birthdays, etc. Send a card or word of congratulations when an important event occurs in their lives. Such thoughtfulness will help you build better relationships.

3. Communication

Business etiquette involves communicating effectively. This includes always returning phone calls and emails. When calling or receiving a call, you should always identify yourself and your department, and speak in a polite and considerate manner. Personalize the conversation with a short question about the other person rather than rushing straight into business. This will help you to make a connection with your caller. When sending an email, use a specific subject line and keep the message businesslike and not overly personal or casual.

4. Dress and Appearance

Good business etiquette includes dressing appropriately. This shows consideration for others, and indicates that you take yourself and your job seriously. An unkempt appearance indicates that you do not care about yourself or respect those around you. When you are unsure what type of dress is required, it is best to err on the conservative side. For work-related social events, do not be afraid to ask what the dress code will be. Remember that even if you are dressing down, such as for a casual Friday, it is still important to practice good grooming.

5. Peers, Subordinates and Superiors

Good etiquette involves showing respect not only to your superiors, but also to your peers and subordinates; in other words, to everyone. If you treat everyone with respect, you will avoid making costly mistakes and experiencing discomfort by accidentally treating a superior in a disrespectful way. A consistently respectful attitude will also build your credibility within the business or industry. Showing respect also means refraining from gossip and from being critical and negative to or about others.

Importance of Business Etiquette

Business etiquette is an integral part of different countries' and regions' business culture. Etiquette encompasses the prescriptive elements of culture—the things people are expected to do and say, or to avoid doing and saying. As the globalization of industries and marketplaces bring managers ever closer to unique cultures around the world, it is more important than ever for managers and small business owners to understand why business etiquette is important.

1. Significance

Business etiquette provides a standard framework within which business people can operate as they communicate and collaborate. Attention to etiquette is a sign of professionalism and respect for others, and it can make positive first impressions while building trust among colleagues. When business partners and co-workers adhere to a well-understood code of etiquette, it can be easier for diverse individuals to work together, focusing their energies on the task at hand rather than trying to understand the cultural eccentricities of others.

Etiquette plays a large role in the business cultures of different countries and geographic regions. An attention to etiquette can help inter-cultural business dealings to be as productive as possible by bringing all parties together under a common understanding.

2. Features

Business etiquette encompasses a range of factors. Verbal and non-verbal communications are a large part of etiquette; communication styles, taboo topics and preferred speaking distances vary by culture. Dress and appearance is another important facet of etiquette. Business people are expected to dress professionally, or at least to take cues from those around them as to what is acceptable. Time sensitivity is another element; some cultures place emphasis on punctuality, and others see punctuality as a sign of eagerness or even hastiness.

3. Types

The art of mastering business etiquette is not reserved for top-level managers visiting foreign business partners. Distinct, yet unwritten, codes of etiquette exist between employees in any workplace, and between customers and employees in the field and on the phone.

Company-level business etiquette looks much the same as intercultural etiquette, with subtle differences arising from the relationship shared by people who work together every day. Etiquette between company representatives and customers look much different; customers are often given the luxury of showing no consideration whatsoever to representatives, while representatives are expected to take courtesy to the extreme with customers.

4. Benefits

An understanding of business etiquette facilitates cross-cultural communication and trade in addition to increasing productivity in the workplace. Bringing managers and small businesses from around the world together can spur innovation and industrial progress through the open sharing of ideas. Collaboration of individuals with diverse experiences and cultural backgrounds can bring the world's brightest minds together by providing a commonly understood framework for social and workplace interaction.

5. Challenges

Small business owners and managers must spend time studying the unique codes of business etiquette of each country or area that they do business in. In addition to this, managers' communication and negotiation styles may become less pronounced as they focus on staying within the boundaries of the local business culture. People in personality-driven businesses, such as sales, can face the largest challenges when forcing different mannerisms or communication styles on themselves.

Text B

Table Manners and Culture Differences

Small-business owners, sales and customer service personnel often assume the role of host or guest at business luncheons, social gatherings and other functions involving food. Regardless of the situation, however, a successful business meal requires close attention to proper business dining etiquette. Manners and conduct are equally important in creating an impression that may affect future attempts at building a long-lasting professional relationship.

1. Hosting Etiquette

Unless there's a specific reason why a luncheon or dinner must held at a certain location, offer a few suggestions and then allow the guest to choose the venue. With a group, select a dining location by majority or consensus. After settling on a location, become familiar with the menu, including house specialties and favorites. Then, covertly supply guests with a budget range by offering, for example, information on house specialties or by suggesting menu items. Plan to arrive at the location a minimum of 15 minutes before any guests are scheduled to arrive. With a group, take the initiative to make any necessary introductions as soon as the entire group assembles.

2. Guest Etiquette Standards

Arrive on time or make sure to contact the host as soon as possible if you're going to be unavoidably detained. Maintain direct eye contact and shake hands during introductions. Increase the chance of remembering an unfamiliar person's name by repeating it aloud when you're being introduced. Be mindful that in a business setting, men and women are peers, so gender-distinguishing behaviors such as holding the door open or pulling out a chair may be viewed as offensive and evidence of poor business etiquette.

3. Table Manners

Table manners refer to the etiquette used while eating, which may also include the appropriate use of utensils. Different cultures observe different rules for table manners. Many table manners evolved out of practicality. If you want to succeed, you'd better watch your table manners since how you handle getting food to your mouth is a big part of your professional image.

4. Dining Etiquette

If you're unsure about what to order, wait for the host to order and then select something similar. Make sure, however, to order foods that are easy to eat rather than barbecued ribs or other finger foods. Begin eating only after the host or the entire group receives their meal. Eat neither slower nor faster than the host or the group. If there's a problem, speak to the waiter or waitress in a courteous, respectful manner. If there's a bone chip or some other undesirable entity in your mouth, remove it with your fork instead of your fingers.

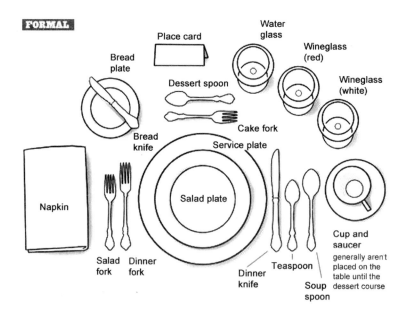

5. The Continental and American Table Manners

There are only two correct styles of eating that the Americans use, but some people eat however it suits them.

With the American style, you hold the fork in your left hand and the knife in your right hand to cut your meat or vegetables. Then you place the knife on the top of your plate with the blade facing in. Next you transfer the fork to your right hand. Now with the fork in your right hand, you take the food to your mouth with the fork tines up.

The difference of continental way is that you keep the fork in your left hand to take the food to your mouth but with the tines down. You can continue to hold the knife in your right hand since you aren't switching the fork over. Just keep it close to your plate. Food is cut the same way for both American and Continental styles, fork in the left hand and knife in the right hand.

6. Reading Menu and Ordering

    1) Starter/Appetizer—Very light seafood (salmon, crabmeat, shrimp…)

        Very small portion of meat (Slice of duck breast or cold meat…)

    2) Soup/Salad—Clear soup (Italian mixed vegetable soup, ox-tail soup)

Cream soup (Mushroom soup, chicken with sweet corn soup)

Vegetable Salad

Sorbet

3) Meat (Steak, Lamb, Duck, Chicken, Pork…)

Seafood (Fish, Prawn, Crabmeat…)

4) Dessert Cake, Fruit, Ice-cream, Cheese

7. Spooning Soup

Spoon the soup toward the center or front of the bowl and then bring the spoon back to your mouth; slurping is considered bad manners in Western etiquette; if the soup is too hot, stir it slightly or simply wait; tip your bowl away from you to retrieve the last spoonful of soup.

8. Breaking Bread

Bread goes on your bread and butter plate which is on your left above the forks; to eat bread, don't bite, but tear off a small piece, butter it if you like and eat it and continue until you are satisfied or have eaten the whole thing.

9. Toasting

Toasting here means to honor someone at a meal or reception by raising a glass of wine, champagne or water and offering a few kind words about that person.

There are two kinds of toasts. There is the informal toast that the host offers at the beginning of the meal to welcome his guests. The host will stand, raise his glass and thank everyone for coming. He will take a sip of his wine. Then the guests, who remain seated, raise their glasses in response and take a sip.

The other is more formal and comes near the end of the meal, usually during dessert. Champagne will be served. After each toast, everyone raises a glass and takes a sip of champagne. It is acceptable etiquette to raise your water glass instead of the champagne flute. You usually just raise your glass to your lips so it appears that you are drinking when you are not. When you make a toasting to your colleague, you could say how good he was to work with, tell a funny story about him, wish him success in his new position or use a favorite quote. Remember you never drink to yourself, only to other people.

10. A Little List of No-No's

1) Purses, briefcases, keys, hats, gloves, eyeglasses …Keep them off the table.

2) Don't salt your food before you taste it.

3) If someone at the table takes a pill, don't ask about it.

4) No food sharing.

5) Do not start eating until all food are delivered to each guest.

6) Don't talk with food in your mouth or folk in your hand and chew with your mouth open.

Cross-culture Sensitivity

Kiss and Hug

Why do some Europeans kiss each other when they say hello? Yes, in some places in Europe such as France, people do give each other a light kiss on the cheek. It's considered friendly and is not sexual in any way. But it's highly unlikely that an American would offer a kiss. Americans seem to like to hug each other frequently. In recent years it has become more popular to hug. But usually it's people who have met before and perhaps haven't seen each other in a while that might hug. At a first meeting, a hug would be very unlikely. I'd say hugging is not usually appropriate in a business situation. Some people are a bit overly friendly.

But if the person initiates it, I'd recommend you grit your teeth and go along with it, otherwise people might think you are rude. So the same rule would apply to getting a kiss from a European: if they initiate it, just go along and be friendly, right? Yes. As the saying goes: "When in Rome, do as the Romans do." In other words: follow the local customs.

No-nos Off-limits

There are a couple of topics that are considered "no-nos" in Western culture. It's best to avoid discussions on politics, religion and money.

Sensitive religion: There are a lot of religions and each one thinks very differently. Overall, it's an area that could cause trouble; so it's best to stay away from it. In some religious centers it's considered impolite to wear hats. Many Western people also think you should remove your hat when dining or in a more formal setting.

Money: In some parts of Asia, discussing salary amounts or how much you paid for something is an acceptable conversation topic, but in the West, people get very uncomfortable when discussing money. Money can be a tricky subject.

Weight: In some Asian societies, when you meet someone and you notice they have put on weight, you might say "Hey! You've gained weight!" But in the West, it's almost never appropriate to comment on someone's appearance. In the West it is viewed as a criticism. So don't comment on age or weight. I think it's best to simply say, "You look well."

Text C

Dress for Business Success

Grooming means dressing well, to be presentable to others. You may want to give a little more attention to how you dress at work because what you wear may be substantially influencing your career path. Although nothing takes the place of talent, hard work, innate ability and ambition, looking your professional best in the work place can give you a competitive advantage. It simply means dressing in a way that projects an image of the sophisticated, successful working individual you are or would like to become.

Business Formal	Business Casual	Smart Casual	Don't
Business Suit Long-sleeved & Collared Shirt Dressed Pant Tie Leather Shoes	Blazer Long-sleeved & Collared Shirt Dressed Pant Khakis pants Leather Shoes (leather sole)	Long-sleeved & Collared Shirt Short-sleeved & Collared Shirt Khakis pants Rubber Sole	T-shirt Tank-Tops Jeans Shorts Tracksuit Flip-lops Sneakers

SHIRTS: As a rule, the simpler the better. Colors: White, pale, blue shirts are preferred; though you may wear dark colored shirts too.

TIES : To play it safe choose a traditional silk tie. No loud colors or patterns.

SHOES: Wear a good pair of leather shoes—black and brown/tan shoes. Shoes must be polished everyday. Do not wear shoes that look casual. Also, do not wear shoes with worn out heels.

BELTS: Wear only formal belts with a sleek buckle. And match your belt to your shoes.

WATCHES: Preferably wear leather strapped watches. If you wear a metal strapped watch, make sure that it fits the wrist well.

Business Formal	Business Casual	Smart Casual	Don't
A two-piece Suit Long-sleeved Shirt Pant Suit (Classic Style) One-piece Dress+ Jacket Leather Sole Shoes	Pant Suit Long-sleeved Shirt One-piece Dress (Long-sleeves or ¾ length sleeves) Leather Sole Shoes	Long-sleeved Shirt + Pants Long-sleeved Shirt + Skirt Twin-set + Pants or Skirt	T-shirt Tank-Tops Jeans Shorts Tracksuits Flip-lops Sneakers

You may wear cheongsam or formal shirt/trousers. You may wear a tunic with a pair of formal trousers. Preferably choose small prints or self colors. Avoid plunging necklines, sleeveless and tight fitting clothes.

SHOES/SANDALS: Shoes with 1½-inch heels are standard. You may wear a pair with smaller heels or a flat pair. Stick with a black/brown pair. Be sure your shoes are polished and that your heels are intact. Do not wear colorful sandals. Avoid heels and sandals with bling. Avoid white colored sandals as they get dirty easily.

BAGS: Apart from your working bag if you are carrying an additional bag, preferably, carry a black or a brown one.

Accessories Earrings: Wear stubs or small rings. Do not wear hoops or dangling earrings

Bracelets/Bangles: You may wear either a bracelet or a bangle. Avoid both. Avoid chunky bracelets or too many bangles.

Case Study

Case One:

Judge which one is proper or improper in the following pictures and list your reasons.

Case Two:

Read the statements about manners in the UK. There are three that are FALSE. See if you can find them. After you have finished it, try to decide on a list of do's and don'ts for good manners in our country.

1) Do stand in a queue when you wait for a bus or to pay for something in a shop.
2) Don't spit on the street.
3) Do burp loudly after a meal.
4) Don't apologize for you bump into somebody on the street.
5) Do say "please" and "thank you" at every opportunity.
6) Don't cover your mouth when you yawn or sneeze.
7) Don't greet people with two kisses.
8) Don't pick your nose in public.

Case Three:

Distinguish which one is Chinese table manner and which one is American table manner and which are shared both. Give your reasons.

1) Not rude to reach in front of someone to grab something.

2) Polite to reach for food with chopsticks.

3) If something is out of your reach, you ask politely for someone to pass it to you.

4) Begins with a set of at least four cold dishes.

5) Business is not always discussed during a meal.

6) Your host will fill up your dish if it is empty.

7) Courteous to hold the door open for male and female.

8) Food is passed around the table.

9) Arrive 30 minuets before your guests.

10) Return the favor.

Notes

1. Netiquette

Netiquette means good behavior on the Internet. It also means to write an e-mail in a proper way with attachment. Before you hit the send button, check your spelling, grammar, punctuation and word choice. Sloppiness gives people a bad impression and is disrespectful to others. When mistakes are found, correct them and resend the e-mail. Typing in all capital letters seems that you are shouting, or typing in all lower keys are like chatting with your friends.

2. Cubicle Etiquette

Working in cubicles can be challenging. Whether you are on the phone or have someone in your cubicle, speak softly. Just because an office doesn't have a door does not mean you can barge in anytime you please. You need to ask permission before entering someone's cubicle. If a colleague is on the phone, you should come back later.

It is a simple matter of respecting the privacy of others.

3. Handshake Etiquette

Exchanging handshakes is a vital part of doing business. Refusing to shake hands is an insult. If you are unable to shake hands because of illness or injury, apologize and explain immediately.

People form opinions about a person from his handshake. There is only one proper handshake and that is a firm handshake.

Extend your hand, make sure the web of your hand makes contact with the web of my hand, close your thumb over the back of his hand; give a slight squeeze with your fingers; two quick pumps and let go.

Useful Words

1. Welcome dinner / Luncheon 欢迎餐宴/午宴
2. Buffet dinner/Luncheon 自助餐
3. Return dinner 答谢宴会
4. Farewell dinner 告别宴
5. Cocktail party 鸡尾酒会
6. employee morale 员工士气
7. professional presence 职业化外表
8. conference table diagrams 会议桌安排
9. office courtesies 办公礼仪
10. sensitive religion 敏感的宗教问题

Useful Expressions

1. Host a dinner/banquet/luncheon in honor of …
2. Welcome dinner / Informal dinner / Luncheon / Light meal / Working luncheon Buffet dinner / luncheon / Return dinner / Farewell dinner / Glee feast / Reception / Cocktail party
3. Please have a seat. Enjoy this happy get-together. Help yourself please.

4. Please yourself at home./Please enjoy yourself.
5. At this point, I propose a toast: to the cooperation between … and … , to the health of Senator…, cheers!
6. Lastly, taking up this glass of fine wine, I propose a toast to …
7. I'd ask you to raise your glass and join me in a toast to the health of all our friends here.
8. Ladies and gentlemen, good evening. The concert/show would start soon. Please get yourself seated. Thank you.
9. On the occasion of the season, I would like to extend season's greetings.
10. Wish you the very best of luck in your job, every success in your future endeavors, good health and a happy family!

Supplementary Materials

Business Etiquette in Paris

Conducting business abroad requires much more than doing the same thing you do in your home market. In Paris, France, there's the added difficulty of a potential language barrier and a significantly different social and business culture. Lack of awareness of Parisian business etiquette could cause the unwary business traveler to unwittingly offend a prospective buyer or investor. Sticking to a few simple guidelines can help you avoid embarrassing mistakes.

1. Be Polite

The French in general and Parisians in particular, are always polite and formal in their verbal communications with colleagues and business contacts. Known as "politesse," different levels of politeness are rigidly respected. Always use "vous," the respectful form of "you," when addressing business contacts; avoid using slang terms. Never use the less formal "tu," the form of "you" reserved for family, close friends, acquaintances and children, unless you are invited to do so. You also should address business contacts as "Monsieur," "Madame" or "Mademoiselle" until you are given permission to address them by their names. Always say "please" — s'il vous plait — and "thank you" — merci.

2. Say Hello

Saying hello properly is important in France. A simple "Bonjour, Monsieur" or "Madame" is expected before entering any discussion. It is also customary to shake hands, though don't overdo your grip; a short, light shake is typical. Once you get to know your business contacts better, it may be acceptable to kiss your counterpart on the cheek. In Paris, this is known as "la bise" and one kiss on each cheek starting on the left is the norm; though it's more like brushing cheeks than actual kisses.

3. Stay Professional

French culture is quite reserved compared to U.S. culture, and you shouldn't make the mistake of discussing your private life during business meetings. Never ask a Parisian business contact about his private life as this is considered rude and intrusive. This is true for long-standing colleagues as well as new contacts. Talk instead about culture, art, politics, movies or anything else topical but impersonal.

4. Dress for Business

Paris is one of the world's most stylish cities and this extends into the everyday wardrobe of professional life. While workplace fashion is increasingly common in the U.S., the French adhere to a culture of formal business attire at all times. A smart, formal suit worn with a shirt and tie tends to be the norm for men, with women equally well dressed in two-piece skirt or pants suits. Good grooming—for example, a stylish haircut—is expected too, while the concept of "dress-down Friday" has little credence in Paris.

5. Take Your Time

You'll never hurry a French business partner into a quick decision; adjust your expectations accordingly. Equally important is to avoid high pressure sales techniques as these are frowned upon. Business in Paris can take longer than you would ever expect, but patience brings its reward. Expect plenty of probing questions and frequent interruptions as well; this is a sign of interest in you and what you're selling so take encouragement from such behavior.

6. Table Manners

Paris is a culinary hot spot, and frequently, business is done over long lunches or dinners; you may be unaccustomed to such formal dining as part of doing business. Most meals include bread, wine and water on the table; never top up your own wine if you are a guest. Always keep your hands visible on the table, never put them in your lap and start eating only when your host asks you to do so.

Questions:

1. *How do you understand the phrase "dress-down Friday"? What is a good grooming in Paris?*
2. *What are the differences of business etiquette between China and Paris according to the text?*

Assignments

1. Translate the following paragraphs into Chinese, and try to understand the basic etiquette.

First impression is very important since you never get a second chance to make a first impression. Hair should be well maintained. Unshaved look does not work for others. Ties should be correctly tied. Pants should not drag on the floor. Shoes should be polished and in good condition. Never wear white sox.

Business manner is different from social introduction manner, because it is based on hierarchy, rank and authority. The rule is that people of less authority are introduced to people of greater authority. Gender and Age play no role. However, there are exceptional cases: Clients and Officials are always more important than people in your company (CEO).

2. **Discuss the following situation with your partner and role play it.**

You're going to visit Mr. Smith, the purchasing manager of an American company. You're supposed to take a business gift. Mr. Smith is a middle-aged man who loves Chinese art. Please find a proper business gift for him and tell your reasons. And you should role play the visit with your partner.

3. **Write a dialogue to give your younger sister suggestions of dressing at different situations. She is a newly graduate. She's usually dressed in casual clothes.**

4. **What will you do to host your important client? Will you tip the head waiter?**

5. **What behaviors of your roommate do you hate most?**

Unit Three
Business Advertising

Objectives

To understand and appreciate the significance, functions and characteristics of advertising.

To learn some theme-related words, expressions, and sentences.

To learn how to advertise products through case study.

To discuss and present ideas about business advertising.

Lead in

1. What advertised products do you have in your daily life? Where can you find advertisements?
2. What is your favorite advertisement? What is the advertisement you dislike most? And why?
3. Which powerful advertising campaign do you know about? Say something about it.

Some Classic Advertising Slogans:

1) Time is what you make of it. (Swatch)
2) Start Ahead. (Rejoice)
3) A diamond lasts forever. (De Bierres)
4) Fresh-up with Seven-up. (Seven-up)
5) Connecting People. (Nokia)
6) Communication unlimited. (Motorola)

7) Focus on life. (Olympus)
8) Behind that healthy smile, there's a Crest kid. (Crest toothpaste)
9) Good to the last drop. (Maxwell)
10) To be No.1 (Erke)
11) Just do it. (Nike)
12) Ask for more. (PepsiCo)
13) Impossible is nothing. (Adidas)
14) Anything is possible. (Lining)
15) Keep moving. (Anta)

Text A

Introduction to Advertising

Advertising is a paid-form presentation or promotion of goods and services. It is non-personal in nature, and the promoter must be identified. Advertising's role is to create a positive image of a product or service by influencing the behavior of target customer.

American Marketing Association (AMA) defines advertising as "the non-personal communication of information usually paid for and usually persuasive in nature about products, services or ideas by identified sponsors through the various media."

Advertising is a form of communication intended to persuade the audience (viewers, readers or listeners) to purchase or take some action upon products, ideas, or services. It includes the name of a product or service and how that product or service could benefit the consumer, to persuade a target market to purchase or to consume that particular brand. These messages are usually paid for by sponsors and viewed via various media. Advertising can also serve to communicate an idea to a large number of people in an attempt to convince them to take a certain action.

The Classification of Advertising

The process of finding a proper position for advertisements is classification. We must analyze the features of different kinds of advertisements, in order to find a proper position for our own advertisement, and choose methods fit it best. The advertisements can be classified into several groups by factors as ultimate goal, target audience, medium, appeal model and the intended effects.

1. By ultimate goal

It is on the basis of the sponsor's general objectives: commercial and non-commercial. A commercial advertisement promotes goods, services, or ideas for a business with the exception of making a profit. A noncommercial advertisement is sponsored by or for a charitable institution, civic group, or religious or political organization.

2. By target audience

Target audience include two aspects, one is the consumer advertising, most of the advertisement we see in the mass media; for example, television, newspapers, radio, magazines are consumer advertisements. The other is business advertising, it is often said to be invisible because unless you are actively involved in some business, you are not likely to see it. In this little part, it includes industrial, trade advertising, professional advertising and farm advertising.

3. By medium

Advertising can be classified on the basis of medium used on transmitting the massage. For example, television, newspapers, radio, magazines, out-of-home, Internet, and direct mail, etc.

4. By appeal model

We can classify advertising according to the following criteria: appeal model. Appeal models in the language of advertising refer to the ways of persuasion. There are two categories: rational appeal and emotive appeal, which respectively make for so-called hard-sell adverts and soft-sell adverts. By rational appeal, the adverts persuades not by appealing to their emotions but by listing hard facts in the form of detailed or specific information, such as quality, convenience, workmanship, effects and so on, whereas the soft-sell, the ad resorts mainly to appealing to emotional motives, so the language concentrates on not facts, but on creating a mood, evoking a desire or satisfying a wish. Nowadays, very few advertisements are strictly hard-sell. Most are a mixture of the two.

5. By the intended effects

By the intended effects, advertisements are classified as immediate action advertising, and awareness and image advertising. Ultimately, the success of advertising rests on whether it influences behavior. Product advertisers want consumers to buy their product, political advertisers want voters to vote their candidate, and sponsors of public-service announcements related to the harmful effects of smoking want the incidence to smoking to decline.

Functions of Advertising

In addition to the definitions and classifications of advertising, we should know the function of advertising in society. In many opinions, advertising acts as a bridge between consumers and producers, between society and trade, between culture and the world.

Advertising, as a tool of the mass-marketing system, is one of the major forces that have helped improve the standard of living in this country and around the world. By publicizing the material, social, and culture opportunities of a free enterprise, consumer society, advertising has encouraged increased productivity by both management and labor force. Advertising also meets social needs. Also, advertising has had both positive and negative effects on consumers that have led to important social and legal changes. Basically, advertising fulfills five functions as follows:

1. The marketing function

Along with public relations and personal selling, advertising is one of the vehicles employed by a business to communicate with its customers. It serves as a marketing instrument by helping companies to sell their products or services. By means of advertising, a business conveys its sales intent and consumption concept to customers. Thus, consumers have a wide range of choices.

2. The economic function

There are two major schools of thought concerning the effects of advertising on economy, i.e. the market power school and the market competition school. According to the market power school, advertising is a persuasive communication tool used by marketers to distract consumers' attention from the price of the product. In contrast, the market competition school sees advertising as a source of information that increases consumers' price sensitivity and stimulates market competition.

3. The communication function

The communication of information is one of the basic functions of advertising. As a form of mass communication, advertising transmits different types of market information to help improve the communication between buyers and sellers in the marketplace. In consequence, consumers can be assured that they can get the commodities they want.

4. The educational function

Through advertising, people can learn about new products and services and understand the advancement of society. Therefore, advertising speeds up the adoption of the new and untried products and, in doing so, accelerates technological advances in industry and hastens the realization of a richer life for all. Advertising also reflects a nation's civilization and contributes to a better understanding of various nations' ideologies.

5. The social function

Advertising has a number of social functions. It informs us of new and improved products and teaches us how to use these innovations. It helps us compare products and their features and make wise purchase decisions. It helps increase productivity and raises the living standard.

Objectives of Advertising

What kind of advertisement is successful? *American Marketing Manager's Handbook* points out that an advertisement should achieve four objectives: AIDA, which represents four words — Attention, Interest, Desire, and Action.

Attention—a good advertisement should attract the consumer to direct their attention to the product of it.

Interest—the introduction and publicity of an advertisement should arouse consumers' great interest.

Desire—the publicity of advertising should stimulate consumers' desire to buy the product, and make them realize that this product is just what they want.

Action—the advertising makes consumer to response to the advertising information and evoke them to take the action of purchasing.

Text B

Characteristics of Advertising Language

The wide use of advertising has created a special style of English—advertising English. Its unique features, simple language and immense attraction separate it from other kind of language. In the development of advertising English, this kind of language has formed its own features in several aspects.

1. *Simplicity.* Advertisements adopt simple language. Simplicity leads to direct communication, clear meaning and easy reading.
2. *Originality.* Advertisement writing is the art of creativity and creative work is dominated by novelty, originality and imagination.
3. *Persuasion.* Advertising language must be convincing enough to change people's assumptions, values, opinions, attitudes, emotions, etc. so as to motivate them to take actions.

Frequently Used Advertisement Headlines

A headline plays an important role in an advertisement, since many people may only glimpse at the headline before deciding whether to read it or not. The effectiveness of any advertisement depends on its headline in a great extent. The headline refers to the sentence(s) in the leading position of the advertisement—the words that will be read, that draw the most attention. Though usually in the form of a brief sentence or just part of a sentence, it is normally placed in the most eye-catching position and given an interesting form.

A headline has numerous functions. The crucial role that the headline should be played is attracting the reader's attention. An effective headline must bring out the most outstanding features of a certain product or service and at the same time must be impressive and easy to remember. Generally speaking, the following 7 categories can be classified according to the efficiency of the headline.

1. *Benefit headline*   Washing makes it better, not smaller. (Cross Creek)
2. *News headline*   Whirlpool announces the end of the noisy dishwasher. (Whirlpool)
3. *Intriguing headline*   Cleans your breath when it cleans your teeth. (Colgate)
4. *Directive headline*   Use Zanol every time you have a headache. (Zanol)
5. *Testimonial headline* Minolta simplifies my life. (Minolta EP50)
6. *Emotional headline*   For the new year, send your love around the world. (Christmas kid fund)
7. *Selective headline*   Zoo visitors please remember: ugly animals like being looked at, too. (San Diego Zoo)

Rhetoric in Advertising

In order to attract consumers' attention and encourage their purchasing desire, rhetoric advertisements are needed. All kinds of rhetoric used in advertising language make language vivid, concise, humorous, novel and full of rhythm, and also bring charm to advertising language.

1. Simile & Metaphor

Simile is a figure of speech in which two essentially unlike things are compared, often in a phrase introduced by like or as. Metaphor is a figure of speech in which a word or phrase that ordinarily designates one thing is used to designate another, thus making an implicit comparison.

    e.g. Light as a feather. (Glass)

        Time is money. (Xerox)

2. Parallelism

The value of parallel structure goes beyond aesthetics. It points up the structure of the sentence, showing readers what goes with what and keeping them on the right track. Parallelism has the potential to create rhythm, emphasis and drama as it clearly presents ideas or action.

    e.g. I don't know who your company. I don't know your company's product.

        I don't know what your company stands for. I don't know your company's record.

        Now what was it you wanted to tell me?

        Moral: Sales start before your salesman calls—with business publication advertising.

3. Pun

Pun is a play on words, sometimes on different senses of the same word and sometimes on the similar sense or sound of different words.

    e.g. Make Time for Time. (Times)

4. Personification

Personification is a figure of speech in which inanimate objects or abstractions are endowed with human qualities or are represented as possessing human form. The use of personification in advertising will endow the product with human emotion, and will make them amicable to consumers.

    e.g. Unlike me, my Rolex never needs a rest. (Rolex)

5. Hyperbole

Hyperbole is a rhetoric that focuses on emotion, and deliberately exaggerates the truth, expresses things higher, stronger and more focused than fact.

    e.g. We have hidden a garden full of vegetables where you'd never expect. In a pie. (Food)

6. Rhetorical question

By arousing curiosity, rhetorical questions motivate people to try to answer the question that is posed. Consequently, people pay closer attention to information relevant to the rhetorical question.

    e.g. "I lost my wallet somewhere in London. Can I still charge my room so I don't have to share a park bench with the pigeons?" Yes. Diners Club provides emergency charging privileges.

    e.g. You're doing all you can to help prevent heart attacks and osteoporosis. Shouldn't you be doing all you can to help preserve your eyesight? The world's leading eye doctors are increasingly convinced: Lutein is essential for your health. Isn't your eyesight too precious not to take Ocutive Lutein?

7. Repetition

In some advertisements, the copywriters often use the method of repetition to stress certain information.

    e.g. Soft curl. Soft color. Soft touch. Permasoft. (Shampoo)

8. Rhyme

Rhyming is correspondence of terminal sounds of words or of lines of verse.

    e.g. My goodness! My Guiness! Hi-fi, Hi-fun, Hi-fashion, only from Sony. (Sony)

9. Contrast

It can deeply reveal and expose the opposition and conflict between things, and emerge the contrast in readers' mind. Making use of contract can make language concise and harmony.

    e.g. No problem too large. No business too small. (IBM)

Case Study

Case One:

Read the following advertisement and distinguish which rhetoric is applied in it.

The Motorover

Stuck at home? Need a better wheelchair? The motorover could be the answer, whether you just want to move more easily about the house or if you want to go out,

Unit Three Business Advertising

visiting friends or shopping.

Unless you want to go up steep hills or stairs, the motorover will take you almost anywhere... You can use it as a chair or a vehicle. You can even fold it up neatly to put into the car. And don't worry about coming in to look at the Motorover, at your request a member of our highly trained sales team will visit you at home with one for you to test drive free of charge.

Call free phone: 0800 500 600 and we will send you more details.

Remember: For ease and convenience, the Motorover is unbeatable!

Case Two:

Appreciate the following ads. And try to answer the following questions.

1. What can you see in this ad? What is the ad for? How do you know? Is it easy to tell?

2. Is the ad effective? How? Does it make you want to buy this product or service?

Public Service Advertisements

Commercial Advertisements

Case Three:

There are different brands of shampoo, which one do you prefer and why?

> **Notes**

1. What advertising can do for your business:

    1) Remind customers and prospects about the benefits of your product or service.

    2) Establish and maintain your distinct identity.

    3) Enhance your reputation.

    4) Encourage existing customers to buy more of what you sell.

    5) Attract new customers and replace lost ones.

    6) Slowly build sales to boost your bottom line.

    7) Promote your business to customers, investors and others.

2. What advertising can't do for your business:

    1) Create an instant customer base.

    2) Cause an immediate sharp increase in sales.

    3) Solve cash flow or profit problems.

    4) Substitute for poor or indifferent customer service.

    5) Sell useless or unwanted products or services.

Unit Three Business Advertising

3. Appreciate the following vocabulary sentences, and focus on the phrases.

   1) The company had a new product to sell so it decided to run an ad to get some business.
   2) Many adverts are only effective because they persuade people that they need products or services when in reality they don't.
   3) Sometimes advertising is deceptive; you can't believe a word they tell you.
   4) Many people try to keep up with the Jones', so they are often very keen for people to see them buying the latest things.
   5) Some of the claims made in TV adverts are implausible; I'll never know how people feel for them.
   6) The company had just enough money in their budget to buy a slot on prime time TV, but only for ten seconds.

Useful Words

1. above-the-line advertising 线上广告
2. account executive(AE) 客户经理
3. advertising agency 广告代理商
4. advertising campaign 广告活动
5. airport advertising 机场广告
6. audience composition 受众构成
7. audio-visual advertising 视听广告
8. insertion order 广告订单
9. mail order advertising 邮购广告
10. recruitment advertising 招聘广告

Useful Expressions

1. Let's go all out on this one. I want a national advertising campaign.
2. Put a full-page ad in the newspaper every Friday, advertising the weekly special coming up.
3. Let's get 20,000 flyers printed. We'll hand them out at the shopping mall next weekend.

4. I want this advertisement to be a testimonial from the gold medal winner. Call her to see if we can get her to endorse our product.
5. We need a new slogan. The old one's not catchy enough.
6. If we want to try door-to-door sales, we'll need professional sales people to make an effective sales pitch.
7. Why don't we do some comparative advertising? Our product is definitely better than the competition's.
8. We need a high-profile television slot. How about the Super Bowl?
9. Can we interest you in a beautiful traveling place? It keeps you feeling and looking young.
10. All the smart money is going on. This is a very popular item.

Supplementary Materials

Larry Page's Speech on Google I/O 2013

Larry Page

I'm really excited to be here. First I want to start with a story. I was very, very lucky growing up, and I was thinking about this as we were preparing for Google I/O. My dad was really interested in technology. And I was just remembering, he actually drove me and my family all the way across the country to go to a robotics conference, and then we got there, and he thought it was so important that his young son go to the conference—one of the few times I've seen him really argue with someone, to get someone in who was underage—successfully, into the conference, and that  was me. Technology should do the hard work so that people can get on with the things that make them the happiest in life.

And one of the themes I just wanted to talk to you about is how important it is for developers here in the room and watching to really focus on technology and get more people involved in it. And also thinking about my dad. His degree, he was lucky enough to get a degree in communication sciences. And you might ask, what the heck is communication science? That's what they called computer science when computers were a passing fad. Sounds kind of funny now, right? I bet that there was a time when that was true.

And I think everyone today is excited about technology. You know, we don't have to worry about that so much anymore. And I think Android and things like that are being adopted much faster than anything else in the past. I look at the rate of adoption of those things, on any basis, are much, much faster. And it's incredible. I pull out my smart phone; it's amazing what we have in the smart phones. We have almost every sensor we've ever come up with. You know, I recently got a scale, and it measures air quality, and it uploads it to the Internet. I'm sure those things will end up in your smart phone, right? That's amazing. And your phone can talk to anyone in the world, almost anywhere in the world.

I was talking to my teams about this. You take out your phone, and you hold it out, it's almost as big as the TV or a screen you're looking at. It has the same resolution as well. And so if you're nearsighted, a smart phone and a big display are kind of the same thing now. Which is amazing? Absolutely amazing?

So I think we also have a lot more devices that we use interchangeably. We use tablets, phones, laptops, and even the Google Glass. All those things we're using. And that's why we put so much focus on our platforms on Android and Chrome. It's really important in helping developers and Google build great user experiences across these devices. To have these platforms. And I'm tremendously excited about all the innovation that you're bringing to life.

Technology should do the hard work so that people can get on with the things that make them the happiest in life. Take search, for example. Perfect search engine, as Amit mentioned, is the "Star Trek" computer, right? Can understand exactly what you meant, can give you exactly what you wanted. And our Knowledge Graph, which you saw, really brings this a lot closer.

I think Google Now, which Johanna just demonstrated, gives you information without even having to ask. And it understands the context of what you talked about before, so you can use things like pronouns, it's amazing. Flight times, your boarding passes, directions, next appointment, all with no effort. Think about a really smart assistant doing all those things for you so you don't have to think about it. You saw how easy some of those experiences felt. And we're just getting started.

The opportunities we have are tremendous. We haven't seen this rate of change in computing for a long time. Probably not since the birth of the personal computer. But when I think about it, I think we're all here because we share a deep sense of optimism about the potential of technology to improve people's lives, and the world, as part of that.

And I'm amazed every day I come to work, the list of things that needs to be done is longer than the day before. And the opportunity of those things is bigger than it was before. And because of that we, as Google, and as an industry—all of you—really only have one percent of what is possible. Probably even less than that.

We should be building great things that don't exist. Right? Being negative is not how we make progress.

And despite the faster change we have in the industry, we're still moving slow relative to the opportunities that we have. And some of that, I think, has to do with the negativity. You know, every story I read about Google, it's kind of us versus some other company, or some stupid thing. And I just don't find that very interesting. We should be building great things that don't exist. Right? Being negative is not how we make progress. And most important things are not zero sum. There's a lot of opportunity out there. And we can use technology to make really new and really important things to make people's lives better.

I think back to a very long time ago. All of humanity was basically farming or hunting all the time. And if you lived at that time, you probably hoped that you could feed your family. And unfortunately that's still true for a lot of people in the world. But certainly for us, we don't worry about that. And the reason for that is technology. We've improved how we grow food and so on, and the technology has allowed people to focus on other things if they choose. By the way, I think being a farmer is great if that's what you want to do. But it's not great if that's what you have to do. And that's what technology lets us do, is free up ourselves to do more different things.

And I'm sure that people in the future will think we're just as crazy as we think everyone in the past was in having to do things like farming or hunting all the time. So to give an example of this, Sergei and I talk about cars. He's working on automated cars now. And imagine how self-driving cars will change our lives, and the landscape.

More green space, fewer parking lots, greater mobility, fewer accidents, more freedom, fewer hours wasted behind the wheel of a car. And the average American probably spends almost 50 minutes commuting. Imagine if you got most of that time back to use for other things. And unfortunately in other countries the commute times are still pretty large. Not as large as the U.S. but still pretty significant.

Today we're still just scratching the surface of what's possible.

Now to get there, we need more people like you, more kids falling in love with science and math at school, more students graduating from school with science and engineering degrees, and more people working on important technological problems. And it's why Google got involved with the movie "The Internship". I'm not sure we entirely had a choice, but they were making a movie and we decided it would be good to get involved. Laurie is up front, she's really responsible for that. And I think the reason why we got involved in that is that computer science has a marketing problem. We're the nerdy curmudgeons. I don't know about you, but that's what I am. Well, in this movie the guy who plays the head of search is by far the coolest character in the movie. And we're really excited about that.

So today we're still just scratching the surface of what's possible. That's why I'm so excited Google's really working on the platforms, in support of all of your innovations. I can not wait to see what comes next. I got goose bumps as I was watching some of the presentations here. And I really want to thank you for all of your contributions. So with that I'm going to do something kind of unconventional and try to take some questions, actually, from all of you…

There're over one million people watching this live over YouTube. It's unbelievable. So let's thank them for participating.

Questions:
1. *What does the story at the beginning of the speech imply?*
2. *Why did Google get involved with the movie "The Internship"? In the movie, who moved you most?*
3. *What do you get from Larry Page's Speech? And what kind of virtues do you find in Larry Page?*

商务英语入门 Introduction to Business English

Assignments

1. Translate the following slogans and enjoy their rhetoric.

Flowers by Interflora speak from the heart. (Interflora)

She works while you rest. (Washing Machine)

Where there is a way, there is a Toyota.

Big thrills. Small bills. (Taxi)

Breakfast without orange juice is like a day without sunshine.

Extraordinary Cola. Extraordinary Choice.

Make yourself heard. (Ericcson)

Live well, snack well. (Snack wells)

Forever elegant chateau figeac. (French red wine)

To me, the past is black and white, but the future is always color.

Where there is a way for car, there is a Toyota.

2. Enjoy the following ads and try to imitate their advertising strategies in the given situation.

1) Digital camera

Say cheese! With the Pixus 2000! Amazing photos with this simple and easy to carry digital camera from Pixus. You'll get the sharpest images even when your subject is moving. Great for photographs of kids and animals. The Pixus 2000 comes with a fashionable carry case and extensive software to make managing your photos as easy as smiling. Amazing value for money!

2) Toothpaste

Keep your smile right with Dazzle Bright! You don't have to give up your morning coffee to say goodbye to those ugly yellow stains on your teeth. Simply change your brand to Dazzle Bright and in seven days see your smile brighten. Developed in our laboratories Dazzle Bright is the most advanced dental formula on the market today. Try Dazzle Bright for one week. Bright teeth or your money back!

3) Car

Own the Road. Cool, sleek, and stylish, the new Hunter from Advanced Motors is the most progressive car on the road today. The Hunter's speed and power are obvious from its futuristic looks but under the surface is a practical and reliable vehicle that will keep you and your family safe.

   4) Soup

   Go for Gold! Keep your kids healthy and warm on those cold winter days. Get some Golden Soup inside them and they'll have enough energy for the rest of the day. With real pieces of chicken breast and fresh vegetables, Golden Soup is the best way to keep them happy.

3. Design an English slogan for our school.

   Step 1: It would be a good idea to … who …

   Step 2: We should … and give…

   Advantage(s): informative/persuasive/humorous

   Disadvantage(s): not persuasive/boring/not distinctive

   Step 3: I suggest we… We can … using it too. Then we can …the top of the ad in big print…

4. Design a print advertisement and describe a new model with no less than 100 words.

   Task: Rejoice series used to be dominant in Chinese shampoo market. However, with the fierce competition, it lost its leading position. How to update its image and enlarge its sales? Write a print advertisement to introduce the new slogan and the updated product. (Headline, body copy and a new slogan should be included.)

5. Design a print advertisement for P&G recruitment.

   P&G is now looking for Year 2014 fresh graduates to join our company as HR trainees (human resource trainees). We believe that we are in a very good position to offer you a variety of career options across our Business Units and Functions.

   Position: HR trainee

   Requirements:

   • Outgoing personality and teamwork spirit.

   • Customer friendly attitude and good communication skills.

   • Quick learner with excellent execution skill and Superior written & oral English is a plus.

   • Microsoft office talent is a plus.

Business English Conversation

Unit Four

Objectives

To understand business English conversation theory.
To raise awareness of some techniques for maintaining a conversation.
To analyze the questions that can be used to keep conversations going.
To conduct business conversations. (Advanced level).

Lead in

1. What is business English conversation theory? How should we conduct a successful conversation?
2. Do you know how to make a formal introduction in business? Have you ever been involved in any business situations? If yes, what were they?

Text A

Business English Conversation Theory

Cooperative Principle People have a common desire to understand each other in communication. In order to reach the goal—they are often cooperative with each other in their conversation. It is believed that in human communication the speaker and the hearer usually cooperate with each other with a common desire to mutually understand each other in their interlocutions. To keep on a successful communication, both the speaker and the hearer, therefore, observe some cooperative principles. However, for some reasons or purposes, people may not always observe these cooperative principles.

H.P. Grice in 1967 suggested that cooperative principle includes the following four maxims: Maxim of Quality, Maxim of Quantity, Maxim of Relation, Maxim of Manner:

Maxim of Quality
    1) Be Truthful.
    2) Do not say what you believe to be false.
    3) Do not say that for which you lack adequate evidence.

Maxim of Quantity
    1) Quantity of Information.
    2) Make your contribution as informative as is required (for the current purposes of the exchange).
    3) Do not make your contribution more informative than is required.

Maxim of Relation
    1) Be relevant.
    2) Do not act too closely.

Maxim of Manner

1) Be Clear.

2) Avoid obscurity of expression.

3) Avoid ambiguity.

4) Be brief (avoid unnecessary prolixity).

5) Be orderly.

Politeness Principles   Apart from the Cooperative Principle, which is taken as the general guidelines to successful human communication, there are other principles guiding speech acts, of which the Politeness Principle (PP) draws most attention from people, because politeness is usually regarded as manifestation of human civilization, and it is one of the most effective strategies modulating interpersonal relationship in human communication. One's impolite or rude speech acts would result in offence against other people involved in communication.

Leech proposes the politeness principle (PP), which contains six maxims:

Tact Maxim	Maximize benefit to other, minimize cost to other.
Generosity Maxim	Maximize cost to self, minimize benefit to self.
Approbation Maxim	Minimize dispraise of other, maximize praise of other.
Modesty Maxim	Minimize praise of self, maximize dispraise of self.
Agreement Maxim	Minimize disagreement between self and other, maximize agreement between self and other
Sympathy Maxim	Minimize antipathy between self and other, maximize sympathy between self and other

These maxims of the politeness principle are generally observed in communication in any language community. The speaker often offers more benefit to the hearer and leaves more cost to himself, with the purpose that both of the two sides will feel respected and get good impression from the other.

Text B

Active Listening Keeps Conversation Going

In a business situation, you will probably need to ask as many questions as possible in order to encourage the other person to talk. You should resist the temptation to fill the conversation with your own monologue. You can relax and bring in more of your own stories. A nice strategy is to find things that you have in common with the other person. This is very different from the situation where you should listen and encourage the other person to speak, and keep the conversation focused on that person for as long as he/she feels the need to speak. Of course, listening to another person speaking for too long can be very boring, so if you find yourself in such way, you'll need to find a way out, either by turning the monologue into a dialogue, or simply by making an excuse to walk away. Just make sure you do it in a way that doesn't upset the other person.

Eye contact is very important. If you start looking around the room, it's a clear sign that you're not really listening. You can also show that you are concentrating on the other person's story by furrowing your brow, or tightening the muscles above your nose. Nod your head slowly to show that you are listening. Don't nod too fast, because it makes you look impatient for the other person to finish. You can also try tilting your head at an angle to show that you are curious. Keep your hands still while you are listening, which might help if you're holding something like a cup of tea. And whatever you do, don't fold your arms since it shows that you are closed to what the other person has to say.

All of these listening noises can be good or bad, depending on how you say them (your intonation or tone of voice) and the situation. Neutral sounds such as mmm and uh-huh are safest, as they show you are listening without expressing an opinion. Going on is useful for encouraging the other person to continue. Most of the other listening noises can be said in at least two ways: an emotional way to express surprise (e.g. Really? Wow! A-ha!) or disappointment (e.g. Oh dear, Oh, Oh no!) or in a neutral way, expressing understanding without an emotional judgment. In general, this neutral way is better if you want to encourage the other person to speak. OK, right and I see can show that you're listening, but they are also often used to show that you want to move the conversation forward, i.e. that you have heard enough, so be careful with your intonation.

Of course, the "best way to respond" will depend on lots of factors, such as the personality of the other person and the type of story they have told. But for many people, it can be very annoying to receive advice or criticism, when in fact all they really wanted was someone who would listen to their story. The best way to show that you've really been listening is to paraphrase the most important parts. Another very common mistake is to turn the other person's story into a story about you. As discussed in question, there's a time for finding things in common, and a time for staying quiet and listening. It's better to show that you are trying to understand the other person's feelings rather than relating everything to yourself. Questions are a good way of showing you've been listening, but the speaker may be frustrated if you only ask fact-based questions. It's better to ask about emotions to encourage the speaker to think about the reasons for what happened.

Case Study

Case One: A Business Conversation Between Exporter and Importer

A Taiwan exporter talks with a Canadian importer

Importer: I'm interested in your portable electric heater. But I'd like more information before placing an order.

Exporter: I'd be happy to answer your questions.

Importer: There's one problem I think I ought to mention. How about the energy efficiency rating of the heater?

Exporter: As you know, heaters tend to be high energy users. Our model E22 is no exception. But although this heater is not as energy-efficient as some, it does have the most durable, problem-free electric motor of any heater we've tested.

Importer: That sounds very impressive. You're talking about the motor that powers the blower?

Exporter: Yes, that's right.

Importer: What about safety features?

Exporter: It has an automatic thermostat control which keeps temperatures from reaching unsafe levels. It also has an automatic shut-off switch in case the thermostat should malfunction. The cabinet contains special insulating materials, so even if it comes into contact with flammable materials its heat will not ignite them. This model is made especially for export.

Importer: Do you have any similar, but smaller, heaters?

Exporter: Why don't you have a look at this one? This is our newest heater.

Importer: How large is the fan?

Exporter: It only has a four-inch blade, but it is made to rotate at high speeds. For its size it distributes the heat very rapidly.

Importer: What are the prices on these models?

Exporter: The large model goes for $60.00, and the smaller unit is $25.00.

Importer: Are those prices the lowest you can offer? I don't know if those prices will work for us.

Exporter: We might be able to offer you a 10% cut on your initial order. Ten percent off is about as low as we can go.

Importer: That sounds more in line with what we can handle.

Exporter: Well, let me check my figures and get back to you on it.

Questions:

1. What kind of conversation theories are involved in the dialogue?

2. Can you invent a conversation with your classmate: Your company is manufacturing tea, and an American exporter is asking you questions on your products.

Case Two: A Business Conversation Between Staffs in a Company

Talking about boosting sales in the coming year

Mr. Chen (the manager) and Peter (a sales representative) are talking about how to boost sales in the coming year.

Peter: Good morning, Mr. Chen. Your new shirt is rather beautiful.

Mr. Chen: Thank you. My daughter chose it for me.

Peter: That's right. She's made such a right decision. It's very different from my common shirt.

Mr. Chen: Yes. To get back to the topic on promotion, here you got any ideas?

Peter: I think we should make our products known by the Chinese at the very beginning of next year. We can run some more chain shops in some medium-sized cities in China, for instance.

Mr. Chen: Well, I think you are right, but the problem is that our products are somewhat expensive. How about reduce our prices?

Peter: Exactly. I think we need to cut our prices by 15%. Our marketing strategy should be to make small profits but quick returns.

Mr. Chen: <u>I agree with you there</u>. But you know, we only make a small profit at these prices. I'm afraid we are bound to be in the red. As I see it, it's more important to improve

product quality and after-sales service than to reduce prices.

Peter: I take your points. On one hand, we need to do further advertising and promotion. On the other hand, we should reduce our after-sales service.

Mr. Chen: I think we should make more advertisements which people can know more about our products.

Peter: That's right. But it will cost us more capital.

Mr. Chen: The more you give, the more you get.

Peter: I agree with you. What's more, we need good sales representatives in China.

Mr. Chen: Yes, if we find good sales representatives, they will make our company more famous in China. Also, they will bring more profit in the future. So I give this assignment to you. Don't let me down.

Questions:

1. According to Conversation Theory, why does Peter say "Your new shirt is rather beautiful"?
2. Pay attention to the underlined parts, do you think they really agree with the former one? Why do they say so? What kind of principle is involved here?
3. Make a similar conversation with your partner based on the situation: David—manager of your company's cooperating firm will visit your factory next Monday; you are required to accompany him and to introduce him about your factory.

Case Three: Meeting at the Airport

A: Excuse me, Sir. Are you Mr. Whiter from New York? I'm Liu Mei, from Guangzhou Textile Import & Export Corporation; I've come to meet you. Welcome to Guangzhou, Mr. White. Our manager will come to greet you later at the hotel. Did you have a pleasant trip?

B: Yes, I enjoyed it very much.

A: Anyhow, it's a long way to China, isn't it? I think you must be very tired.

B: But I'll be all right by tomorrow and ready for business. Do you know where the baggage claim area is?

A: How many pieces of luggage do you have? I wish you a pleasant stay here.

B: Thank you for meeting me at the airport.

A: If all is ready, we'd better start for the hotel.

Case Four: Airport Departure

A: It's very kind of you to come and see me off.

B: It's a pity that you're leaving so soon.

A: I'm very grateful to you for your warm hospitality.

B: What is your flight number?

A: It's Flight No.302, Northwest Orient Airlines. Thank you very much for everything you have done for me during my stay in Britain. I must, on behalf of my company, thank you again for your generous help. My wife and I will be looking forward to seeing you when you come to the US.

B: I promise I'll take the first chance to call on you when I get there.

A: I shall miss you very much and thank you for your company. I hear they're announcing my flight over the public address system.

B: Bon voyage, Mr. Andrew. And a safe landing in the States.

Notes

1. Getting down to business

The beginning of a meeting presents a major dilemma: is it better to get straight down to business, or is it important to allow or even encourage small talk? Small talk refers to conversations about things which are not directly relevant to the current task we are doing or the situation we are in. If you want to get down to business straightly, make sure everyone arrives on time. Secondly, get most of the work done before the meeting. That means sending round detailed agendas, with clear instructions for all participants telling them what they need to do to prepare for the meeting. Thirdly, stick to the agenda. Fourthly, set a time limit and stick to it. Of course small talk has its place, but that place is not a meeting.

2. Getting involved in meetings

Many learners of English worry about their mistakes and allow their insecurities to prevent them from participating in meetings fully. Record yourself speaking at a meeting in English. Later, listen to your performance and try to correct some of the mistakes you hear. Learn a few interrupting phrases like "Can I just say something?" or "Sorry to interrupt, but …" These phrases will give you time to plan what you're going to say.

Actively try to involve less confident colleagues by asking their opinions frequently and listening patiently while they speak. Go for it! Speaking English in public is like learning to ride a bike. Ask a colleague what bad habits you have with English grammar or pronunciation. Then try to correct yourself when you're speaking fluently. Learn some phrases for checking understanding and make sure you use them. If somebody interrupts you, give them a chance to speak, especially if you know that person isn't very confident about using English in meetings. If they hesitate, encourage them with phrases like "Go on" or "After you."

3. Brainstorming in the meeting

Brainstorming is one of the most popular techniques used in meetings to generate ideas for solving a specific problem. Alex Osborn, the inventor of the term "Brainstorming," established four rules. Firstly, it's important to focus on quantity. Write everything down, the more ideas, the better. Secondly, participants need to withhold criticism. Never criticize another person's idea during the brainstorming session, as it will prevent people from being creative. There's plenty of time for criticism in the evaluation stage later. Thirdly, we should welcome unusual ideas. Try to challenge your assumptions and ask "what if …?" questions. Finally, try to combine and improve ideas. This is the real power of brainstorming: person A's crazy idea, which would never work in practice, may get person B thinking about a similar idea which might just work. Even better, person A's crazy idea and person C's crazy idea can be combined, taking the best parts of each. So instead of saying "no" or "yes, but …" we need to train ourselves to say.

Useful Words

1. agreement 协定，协议，契约
2. approval 批准，认可，同意，赞同
3. convention 大会；协定，惯例，公约
4. delegate 代表
5. reconcile 和解，调和，妥协
6. agenda 议程表，议事日程
7. alternative 两者择一的，供选择的；非主流的
8. articulate 清楚地讲话，发音
9. settlement 安置；解决；协议；结算；住宅区
10. breakthrough 重大进展；突破

Useful Expressions

1. We are a manufacturer of household appliances.
2. We are the leading exporters of garments in China.
3. We are the China National Textiles Import and Export Corporation, with our headquarters in Beijing. Our company was established in 1985. We have about 1,000 employees.
4. Our sales volume was about 50 million dollars annually. We developed a new assembling system. The machine is durable / small and light/easier to use.
5. Here're some handouts that give a brief introduction of our products. Please take a look.
6. Let me show you around our factory. Our products are less expensive but higher in quality.
7. Our home textiles are made in a great variety of colors. Our products have met with a warm reception in many countries.
8. There are lots of commodities which greatly interest me. You certainly have a great variety of goods on display.
9. We have many patterns and shades for you to choose from.

10. I'm calling to find out how you would like your order of speakers, by air or by sea?

Supplementary Materials

Small Talk Is the Cement That Holds Businesses Together

Small talk is a vital part of working with other people: finding out what they're doing, what they're having problems with, and what they think they should be doing differently. Perhaps even more importantly, it's about getting to know your colleagues and business partners as people, not just as business machines. Business is very largely based on trusting people, helping and being helped by people and persuading people to do things. How can you achieve any of those things if you don't spend time getting to know each other?

When is this relationship-building supposed to happen? Outside of working hours? No, that's not right if we accept that relationship-building is real work. When we're sitting at our computers or in our offices? No, that's when we might need to avoid interruptions and stay focused. So when? A lot of the best small talk happens accidentally: the classic situations are the queue for the photocopier, the coffee machine or the water cooler. But a much more systematic and effective way to build good relationships between people from different departments is to allow small talk to flourish in meetings.

Let's get a few things straight about meetings: the whole point of bringing people

together for meetings is to generate discussion, to resolve misunderstandings, and to find solutions to problems that people couldn't find if they were working alone. If everything is carefully planned in advance, and the chair of the meeting sticks rigidly to the agenda, none of those things can take place. Of course, there's a time when it's appropriate for one person to talk and everyone else to listen and learn, but that's a presentation, not a meeting.

If you're serious about making your meetings more effective, you need to give the participants plenty of time to ask questions, take the conversation in new directions, say things which may or may not be relevant, and above all, get to know each other. Of course, you need to make sure things don't get out of control, but that means finding a sensible balance between small talk and getting down to business.

A company which does not tolerate small talk may get things done more quickly, but that doesn't mean it'll do things the best way, making full use of the skills and ideas of Text B. Its employees … and it may well find that it loses its best employees and its customers just as quickly. Small talk refers to conversations about things which are not directly relevant to the current task we are doing or the situation we are in. Classic examples include discussions at work about the weather, the news, TV programs, family news, etc.. Small talk is small in the sense that the conversations tend to be quite short.

Questions:
1. How does small talk keep conversations going? Do you like small talks with strangers? Is it suitable for a small talk during the meeting?
2. What kinds of gestures do you have in listening to others when interested or uninterested?
3. If you're serious about making your meetings more effective, what will you do to get it?

Unit Four Business English Conversation

Assignments

1. Translate the following two conversations, and role-play them in your group.

1) English to Chinese

An American firm considers using a Chinese factory to manufacture its bicycles.

Manufacturer: How do you do, Mr. Kraft? I've been expecting you.

Businessman: It's good of you to show me around. Your plant is much smaller than I expected.

Manufacturer: Our small size makes us very flexible. As you know, the bicycle business is very much influenced by trends and fashion. Styles change from year to year. Because we're small, we can respond to changes quickly.

Businessman: Yes, you have a good reputation in the field. We've been using a manufacturer in Japan. They are very large and efficient, but they do have trouble getting the new models out quickly.

Manufacturer: We certainly hope we can solve that problem for you.

Businessman: Let's hope so. Well, shall we get started on our tour?

Manufacturer: I suggest we start at the beginning of our production line.

Businessman: Fine. How long have you been in the bicycle business, Mr. Chou?

Manufacturer: I began in 1973.

Businessman: Does your factory carry out the entire process of manufacturing?

Manufacturer: Almost. A few necessary items like lights and seats are made elsewhere. Then they are checked for quality at our factory and added to the bicycles.

Businessman: What kind of quality control do you have?

Manufacturer: It's extremely tight. Quality is one of our primary considerations.

Businessman: Well, thank you for showing me your plant and answering my questions. I'm looking forward to receiving the samples we talked about. If they're as good as I think they'll be, my company will be placing an order soon.

Manufacturer: We'll certainly try to meet your requirements.

2) Chinese to English

林： 请问，您是布莱克先生吗？

陌生人： 哦，不是，你弄错了。

林： 对不起，不过您能告诉我谁是布莱克先生吗？

陌生人： 恐怕不行，你最好问那边那位先生。

林： 对不起，请问您是从美国来的布莱克先生吗？

布： 是的，我是约翰·布莱克，从美国来的。

林： 我是中国纺织品进出口公司郑州分公司的翻译，我姓林。

布： 林先生，您好！

林： 您好！这位是我们的经销部经理王先生，他专程来迎接您。这位是从美国来的布莱克先生。

王： 您好，布莱克先生。这段时间我们一直在盼望着您的到来，现在您终于来了，我们热烈欢迎您。

布： 谢谢。我有机会到郑州来心里真高兴。

王： 我们对您的来访也感到很高兴。我们希望您的访问将促进我们之间的相互了解，并加强我们之间的贸易关系。您坐这么久的飞机一定很累了吧？

布： 哦……不是太累。飞机上的服务真不错。十分舒适愉快。您知道，这是我第一次到中国来，说实话，我路上非常激动。

王： 这真叫我高兴。布莱克先生，咱们先到候机室休息，然后再去取行李和办理手续吧。

布： 好的。

王： 请这边走，布莱克先生。

布： 好，谢谢。

2. Make up a dialogue with your partner according to the following situations.

A invites B to his party by telephone, B accepts the invitation. B is late for the party, so he apologizes to A. A has been promoted to the manager, B is congratulating him. B thanks A for the party, and waves goodbye.

3. In groups, make a call about notice of a large meeting involving people from several departments. Try to role-play the situation. You can use these ideas to help you:

• You are the general secretary of the boss. You need to call the chief of different

departments.
- The meeting is about a new project that will be undertaken next month. Be as specific as possible.
- It is the first of a series meeting and it will take about 2 hours.
- All of them need to get arrived before 8 o'clock.

4. Work in groups of around five people. Choose one person to chair your meeting.

You all work for the same organization. The managers from your head office have asked you to make your premises more suitable for disabled employees and visitors. Some of the ideas that you brainstormed included:
- installing a lift
- adding a wheelchair ramp to the steps outside the front door
- replacing the traditional heavy front door with sliding doors
- training reception staff how to communicate with deaf people
- making the whole building easier and safer for blind people to explore

5. Make a dialogue according to the given situation.

Meeting at the airport: At the customs; Call on a customers; Receiving visitors;

Making an agenda: Changing plans; Before touring a factory; Leading a tour of a factory;

After a tour of a factory: Airport departure; Inquiry; Offer; Counteroffer; Negotiating prices;

Order: Stocks; Delivery; Shipment; Packing; Terms of payment.

Business Negotiation

Unit Five

Objectives

To understand and appreciate the significance of negotiation and business negotiation.
To learn some theme-related words, expressions, and sentences of negotiation.
To learn some relationship building techniques.
To discuss and present ideas about business negotiation.

Lead in

1. What is negotiation? What is a successful negotiation?
2. Have you negotiated with others? If yes, share your experience.

Text A

Business Negotiation

Negotiation is a common human activity as well as a process that people undertake everyday to manage their relationships such as a buyer and a seller, a husband and wife, children and parents. As the stakes in some of these negotiations are not very high, people need not have to get preparations for the process and the outcome. But in international business negotiations, the stakes are usually high. People cannot ignore this fact, so they have to get preplans in a more careful way. Both parties in this kind of negotiation should contact each other so that they can get a better deal rather than simply accepting or rejecting

what the other is offering. The whole process of negotiation is based upon the premise that both parties are interdependent, that is, one side cannot get what he/she wants without taking the other into consideration. In the process of negotiation, there are no rules, tradition, rational methods or higher authorities available to resolve their conflict once it crops up. Negotiation is a voluntary process of giving and taking where both parties amend their offers and modify their expectations so as to come closer to each other and they can quit, at any time.

Negotiation is at the heart of every transaction and, for the most part, it comes down to the interaction between two sides with a common goal (profits) but divergent methods. These methods (the details of the contract) must be negotiated to the satisfaction of both parties. As we will see later that it can be a very trying process that is full of confrontation and concession. Whether it is trade or investment, one party will always arrive at the negotiation table in a position of greater power. That power (the potential for the profits) may derive from the extent of the demand or from the ability to supply. The purpose of negotiation is to redistribute that potential. There is no such thing as "to take it or leave it" in international business. In fact, everything is negotiable. It all depends on the expertise of the negotiators.

An Overall Framework of IBN: International business negotiation (IBN) is a consultative process between governments, trade organizations, multinational enterprises, private business firms and buyers and sellers in relation to investment and import and export of products, machinery and equipments and technology. Negotiation is one of the important steps taken towards completing import and export trade agreements.

To reach the desired results, the negotiators must seriously carry out the relative trade policies of their own countries. They should have good manners and speak fluent English. They should have a profound knowledge of professional technology and international markets. They should know the specifications, packing, features and advantages of the products and be able to use idiomatic and professional terms. In general, an overall framework of international business negotiation covers the following aspects: 1) background factors, 2) the atmosphere and 3) the process.

Text B

Basic Rules of Business Negotiation

Interdependence. "One palm cannot clap." This is true of everyday life, and is also no exception to conducting a business negotiation, in which both sides are locked together on account of their goals. A seller cannot exist unless he has a buyer, which determines this relationship between them.

Concealment and Openness. In many business negotiations, both parties may conceal their real intentions and goals to better their chances of best deal possible. As this is an open secret, smooth communication and good mutual understanding will to some degree become difficult, which does easily lead to misunderstanding. To achieve more satisfactory results, both parties will have to decide how open and honest they should be about personal preferences and needs, and to what extent they should trust the other side.

Different Negotiating Situations. Both parties must change as required of them by situations. If either of them fails to find out which type of negotiation is necessary in a particular situation, the odds (chances) are he will fail.

Bargaining Mix and Creativity. How to make both "sides" meet in negotiations without causing much loss to either, which may bring both out of the win-lose mix and help accomplish their objective, requires creativity. And the discovery of this is based on the environment where negotiators feel cooperative and dedicated to seeking the best solution possible instead of meeting but one side's needs.

Proposal Exchange. The heart of negotiation is the exchange of offers and proposals. There is an unstated assumption in negotiation that both sides will show their exchange of offers to the process of finding a solution by making concessions to the other side's offer. And through the process of offer and counter-offer a point is reached on which both sides will agree. To be successful, a negotiator needs to be able to understand the events that are taking place during the exchange of offers, to know how to use them to advantage, to keep the other side from using them to the negotiator's disadvantage.

Winner or Loser. In the process of business negotiation, if both parties try to reach an agreement that maximizes their outcome, it may lead either party to be concerned about only with his ends and ignore the needs of other side. Such a situation will most probably create problems.

Generally speaking, in a common negotiation the parties involved are either winner or loser, but in a formal international negotiation such a phenomenon will not probably occur just because of the engagement of experts.

Case Study

Here are some real stories happened in life, please think about their background, the atmosphere and the negotiation process.

Case One: In the following case, Mitchell, the buyer, is negotiating with Mr. Zhang, the seller, about the price of Electric Heaters.

Mitchell: What is your price per set for Electric Heaters?

Zhang: Our price is US$ 45 per set FOB Guangzhou. We can supply from stock.

Mitchell: It's a high price. I have another offer for a similar product at a much lower price.

Zhang: I can assure you that our price is most realistic. A trial sale will convince you of what I say.

Mitchell: If you can go a little lower, I'd be able to give you an order right now. You I have here some clients who intend to buy 5000 sets. But the price they allow me is only 40 dollars per set.

Zhang: 40 dollars? This price is absolutely out of the question. You cannot get the goods anywhere at this price.

Mitchell: But 40 dollars is their final bid and I can't help it. I hope you will give it a second thought, 5000 sets is no small figure, is it?

Zhang: Well, since it is a big order, I think I'll allow you a discount of 5%. That is, 42.75 dollars per set. It's quite a bargain. I hope you will appreciate it.

Mitchell: I accept. Thank you for your cooperation.

Zhang: But it will leave us very little margin of profit. I hope our first supply will induce your clients to place regular orders with us in the future.

1. Is it a successful negotiation?

2. Are there any tactical expressions used in this negotiation?

3. What kinds of rules can you learn from it?

Case Two: In the following case, Robert, the buyer, is negotiating with Dan, the seller, about the price of coats.

R: Even with volume sales, our coats for the Exec-U-Ciser won't go down much.

D: Just what are you proposing?

R: We could take a cut on the price. But 25% would slash our profit margin. We suggest a compromise — 10%.

D: That's a big change from 25. 10% is beyond my negotiating limit. Any other idea?

R: I don't think I can change it right now.

Unit Five Business Negotiation

Why don't we talk again tomorrow?

D: Sure. I must talk to my office anyway. I hope we can find some common ground on this.

NEXT DAY

D: Robert, I've been instructed to reject the numbers you proposed; but we can try to come up with some thing else.

R: I hope so, Dan. My instructions are to negotiate hard on this deal, but I'm try very hard to reach some middle ground.

D: I understand. We propose a structured deal. For the first six months, we get a scount of 20%, and the next six months we get 15%.

R: Dan, I can not bring those numbers back to my office. They'll turn it down flat.

D: Then you'll have to think of something better, Robert.

1. Are there any tactical expressions used in this negotiation?
2. What kinds of rules can you learn from it?
3. Who is the winner? Is Robert the winner or loser? Why?

Case Three: The following is a very famous negotiation happened in the movie *American Dreams in China*. The three Chinese are negotiating with an American— Bono. Read it and analyze why it is a successful negotiation.

WANG–Wang Yang; CHENG–Cheng Dongqing; MENG–Meng Xiaojun

WANG:　Mr. Bono. It's your gift, from me.

BONO:　It's got from China Town?

WANG:　Chinese moon cake. Next week is the moon festival. And if the fight breaks out later, I have something to throw.

BONO:　Hahahaha...

WANG:　Oh hoo, you got the joke, for you.

CHENG: Mr. Bone, we officially offer a formal apology, we acknowledge the commodity copyright infringement and prepare to settle.

WANG:　But not fifteen million.

CHENG: Please, pick any clause you want, any clause that is related to our copies.

LADY:　Clause eleven.

CHENG: The WTO Copy rights and performances and phonograms treaties of implementation as of nineteen ninety eight, amended section 101 by added definition of "Geneva Conventions." Pick another one please.

CHENG: This is because I memorized the entire text on the plane coming here. It is a skill that I mastered when I was eighteen. That year, I memorized the whole Xinhua English dictionary. For your information, I was only considering a mediocre of all my peers. Chinese students are extremely adapted at taking exams. You can't imagine what they are willing to go through to succeed. You don't understand Chinese culture.

MENG: Mr. Bono, regardless of the final court decision, this meeting is the start of our formal promotion. We hope EES can inform copyrights in Chinese market. We don't like to be called thief. We've come here today, hoping to educate you about one thing, and China has changed. Unfortunately, you are still stuck in the past.

BONO: Mr. Meng, may I remind you, Yao Ming is in the NBA.

MENG: That's because NBA was trying to tap into China market, China is already the world's largest market for English language education. Today, Chinese students don't expect to stay in America, they want to go home. Yet you're still stuck on whether they cheat on exams.

CHENG: Mr. Bono, before we came to the state, we debated it's best to release the New Dream on the stock exchange. Now, I have come to a decision, New Dream IPO will be officially announced, today.

BONO: What make we should care?

CHENG: But you will care, I will be waiting for the right opportunity for the company to go public. Now, I've got it. That's right; it's you who give us this opportunity. Thank you, Mr. Bono. You are the one who has got us an attention of potential investors from Wall Street. They will see us company with integrity and courage, the more we pay in compensation, the Greater valuation we will get in the future. In addition, there will be at least one more benefit from listing New Dream... Someday, when we are no long teachers. but representatives of the world 's largest educational service corporation. You may finally show us that respect we deserve. We will not have to rely on a lawsuit to communicate with each other. More importantly, I am also doing this for personal reasons, I have a friend who is more brilliant than I have never peered at deserving success. When he came to American, the best man of my generation destroyed here. The place here has never been even. This is my way of regainning my friend's dignity. According to our Chinese proverb, I am like a Tubie—a soft shell of turtle, someone afraid to go out and take risks. Now, I am standing here, terrified even as I speak. But as my friends said, some things are so important that force us to overcome our fears.

1. Any tactical expressions used in this negotiation?
2. What kinds of rules can you learn from it?
3. Whose presentation do you like best? Who is the winner in your mind? State your reason.

Notes

1. Two kinds of usual tactics of negotiation: offensive tactics and defensive tactics

Offensive tactics:

 Ask questions; Tit for tat; Feign a blow to the east and attack in the west;
 Use of commitments; Uncover the counterpart's interests and "the right answer";
 Search for contextual irregularities or discrepancies;
 Be aggressive; Present arguments; The best alternative.

Defensive tactics:

 Minimal response and feigned misunderstanding;
 Silence is golden; Side-stepping; The "yes-but" technique; Counter-question;
 Exposing dirty tricks; To be social; To concede a point on the agenda;
 To reveal no bargaining position at all.

2. Turning new contacts into partners

 We meet dozens or even hundreds of people at conferences, and often find it difficult to remember faces to go with all the business cards we receive. For this reason, we need to do something different, to stand out from the crowd, to give the other person a better chance of remembering who we are and, hopefully, doing some business with us in the future. The simplest approach is to follow up your meeting with an email or connect with them on a social networking site. A much better approach is to try to build a relationship face-to-face. Whatever you do, make sure you try at least. You'll find it gets much easier with practice, and end up with some great new business partners—and maybe some good friends too.

3. Questioning and clarifying

In an important business negotiation, it's vital to have a procedure. Of course, you can deviate from that procedure as much as you like as the negotiation progresses. And certainly the most important parts of the negotiation, trading concessions and clinching the deal, are almost impossible to plan. But the earlier stages definitely can be planned, and both sides will benefit if you take the time to do things properly. Firstly, make sure you include time to build relationships with the other party. The next stage is to establish the procedure, unless you've been really well organized and done this via email in advance of your face-to-face meeting. Then it's time for the first party to present its position. During the other party's position statement, it's absolutely vital for you to say as little as possible. When they've finished their opening position statement, you finally get your chance to speak, but again, you'll benefit a lot more by asking simple questions and letting them talk some more. Just don't be too aggressive in your questioning.

Useful Words

1. adjourn 中止；休会；延期
2. brainstorm 脑力激荡，集思广益
3. concede 容忍；容许；让步
4. agenda 议程
5. announce 通告；宣布；宣告；公之于众
6. articulate 能清楚有力表达思想感情的
7. attorney 律师；辩护律师
8. compromise 妥协；折衷；和解

9. amendment 改善（正）；修正案
10. settlement 安置，解决，协议

Useful Expressions

1. We'd really like you to increase your order by 10%. So we're prepared to cut our prices by 5%.
2. Our price is US$ 45 per set FOB Shanghai. We can supply from stock.
3. It's a high price. I have another offer for similar product at a much lower price.
4. I think I'll allow you a discount of 5%. It's quite a bargain. I hope you will appreciate it.
5. My instructions are to negotiate hard on this deal, but I'm try very hard to reach some middle ground.
6. Well, it's been a pleasure doing business with you. You drive a hard bargain, but I think this will be a good deal for both of us. Here's to a successful long-term relationship!
7. So you said you could be flexible on the initial setting-up fee in exchange for slightly higher monthly fees. We could accept a 1% increase in the monthly fees for the first two years in exchange for a 5% cut in the set-up fee.
8. I'm afraid 1 km is totally out of the question, as is a 2-year term. We might be able to show some flexibility in both of these, for 15 km for a period of four years.
9. As I said earlier, the three-month notice period is as long as I'm prepared to accept, and I also can't accept the non-compete clause as it stands.
10. We might be able to work out something like that, in exchange for a longer notice period.

Supplementary Materials

Negotiations: Relationship-building Techniques

In practice, none of these defensive strategies may be necessary. Most good negotiators understand the importance of creating long-term trust and protecting their reputations, so they'll do their best to keep you happy. This is one reason why used car salesmen aren't as manipulative as we might expect them to be—they have a reputation to build and protect.

Good negotiators build strong long-term relationships. In many ways, this is even more important than the traditional "bargaining" element of negotiations. If you leave the negotiation feeling defeated or cheated, you're not going to want to negotiate with that person again. If you find out later that the other person took advantage of your naivety, again, you're not likely to want to do business with that person. You may even try to get out of the contract you have agreed; in many situations, it is legal and normal to declare a contract null and void if you have been deceived. You're also unlikely to recommend the deceptive negotiator to other friends and colleagues, and you may even go public with the story of your bad experience, which will damage the person's reputation.

But if you do find yourself in a negotiation with a professional manipulator, what can you do to protect yourself? The three keys are awareness, preparation and control. Firstly, simply be aware of the situation and its risks. Think very carefully before making any commitments. Secondly, find out as much as you can before the negotiation, especially concerning prices—what price are other people offering for similar products and services? You also need to research your own needs very carefully, including a deep understanding of what you don't need. Thirdly, make sure you don't lose control. Don't be afraid to walk away from a negotiation if you're not sure, and take time to discuss your concerns with friends and colleagues. Of course, the other negotiator may tell you that you can't go away and think about it, that the decision must be made right here, right now. But that's almost always just a bluff. In a high-stakes negotiation with a professional, a rushed decision is almost always a mistake.

We all negotiate all the time: with our husbands and wives, with our parents and our children, and with our friends and colleagues: What time do the kids have to go to bed? Whose turn is it to go to the supermarket? Can you help me with my presentation? Of course, these situations don't always feel like negotiations, not least because these are all long-term relationships. But they have a lot more in common with professional negotiations than you might think.

It's interesting that this assumption doesn't work when buying a souvenir in a tourist resort, where long-term relationships don't exist—one reason why you need to be especially careful in such situations. It also doesn't really work when you're buying or selling your house or flat—the classic one-off sale with huge potential short-term gains for manipulators. Fortunately, most people aren't naturally manipulative; so again, relationship-building is almost always the best approach.

On the other hand, the situations that we tend to think of as "typical negotiations," such as buying a used car, haggling over the price of an overpriced souvenir in a tourist trap, or selling your flat, are much less typical than they seem. These are all one-off negotiations, where there's no time or need to build long-term relationships. In business, almost all negotiations are long-term. Both the used car salesman and the souvenir seller are using sales techniques (or sometimes manipulation tricks). Of course selling is an important skill in life and business, as is an awareness of the tricks that other people may use. But this isn't really what negotiations are all about.

Next are the following strategies about relationship building.

1. Finding things in common

There's no doubt that we like people who are like us. In other words, if we can identify with them and understand them as people, not just business machines, we're much more likely to want to do business with them. In practical terms, there are two sides to this technique: one is to ask questions to find out about the other person. But just as importantly, we need to be open about ourselves, to help the other person to understand us too.

2. Showing an interest

When the other person is talking about himself/herself, we need to listen carefully and show that we are listening. This means not just making "listening noises" like "I see" and "Really?" but actually being interested in the other person. Remember what they are telling you, so you can bring it up next time you meet (e.g. How's your daughter getting on at university?).

3. Flattery

Say nice things about the other person or their organization. If that person bought you a meal, tell a third person how nice the meal was and how much you enjoyed the conversation. If you've just arrived in their office, say how nice it is. If you notice a diploma on the wall, ask about it and make sure you sound impressed when they tell you. But whatever you do, make sure you sound convincing—there's nothing worse than false enthusiasm!

4. Generosity

Research has shown that if you give something to another person, they almost always feel obliged to return the favor … or even a much bigger favor. Of course, there's a limit: you can't be too cynical and expect someone to knock 10% off their asking price just because you've bought them a nice coffee. But a little genuine kindness can go a long way.

5. Gratitude

Whenever the other person is kind to you, always make sure you say thank-you. It may seem like a tiny detail, and perhaps an obvious one, but in fact it can make all the difference. Just imagine how you'd feel if someone failed to thank you for your own kindness! And when you say thank-you, don't just say "thank-you."

6. Personal touches

This can go both ways. Firstly, show that you're treating the other person as an individual, someone special. That means remembering their name, and maybe organizing something based on the likes and dislikes they've expressed. Secondly, show that they're dealing with you as a person, not just your organization. If you're taking them to your favorite restaurant, make sure they understand that it's not just an anonymous place to eat, but something that you've chosen personally, which says something about who you are.

Questions:
1. How should we establish a business relationship with others? What are the strategies?
2. If you do find yourself in a negotiation with a professional manipulator, what can you do to protect yourself? What are the defensive strategies involved in the negotiation?
3. Did you ever negotiate with your parents, friends or classmates? Share your experiences with us.

Assignments

1. Translate the following conversation into Chinese, and role-play in your group.

D — Dan Smith   R — Robert Liu

D: I'd like to get the ball rolling by talking about prices.

R: I'd be happy to answer any questions you may have.

D: Your products are very good. But I'm a little worried about the prices you're asking.

R: You think we are about to be asking for more?

D: That's not exactly what I had in mind. I know your research costs are high, but what I'd like is a 25% discount.

R: That seems to be a little high, Mr. Smith. I don't know how we can make a profit with those numbers.

D: Please, Robert, call me Dan. Well, if we promise future business, volume sales will slash your costs for making the Exec-U-Ciser, right?

R: Yes, but it's hard to see how you can place such large orders. How could you turn over so many? We'd need a guarantee of future business, not just a promise.

D: We said we wanted 1000 pieces over a six-month period. What if we place orders for twelve months, with a guarantee?

R: If you can guarantee that on paper, I think we can discuss this further.

2. Have a negotiation with your classmate based on each situation given below.

Situation 1

Tenant: You should emphasize the damage of PC is caused by the broken water pipe upstairs and maintaining the building in good shape is the landlord's responsibility. So the landlord should compensate partly for the ruined PC. You can threaten to quit renting but not to go to court, because the contract states clearly that all tenants shall carry their own insurance for personal property.

Landlord: Because the contract you signed with the tenants states clearly that all tenants shall carry their own insurance for personal property, you should insist that the tenant go to the insurance company to get compensation. You are not afraid of going to court or any other threats because you have a lot of potential tenants.

Possible outcome: win-lose negotiation

Situation 2

Customer: You should start with higher price when you sell your old car and begin with a lower price when you buy the car.

Car dealer: You can offer some attractive term when you buy the old car and sell the new at a higher price. But you should remember to keep the customer happy and avoid quarrelling.

Possible outcome: win-win negotiation

Situation 3

Secretary: You can tell the businessperson your boss's schedule at first and you cannot change the arrangement of your boss.

Businessperson: You may concede as to the date of meeting.

Possible outcome: win-win negotiation

Situation 4

The attorney for an angry wife: You can threaten to delay the divorce and publicize his sexual scandal. And you may also concede a little in the marital assets claims. But you need the agreement from your client.

The lawyer for a man: 50% of the marital assets is your bottom line.

Possible outcome: win-win or win-lose negotiation

Situation 5

Mr. Brown: Emphasize the trees on the land in negotiation. If there are more than 80 trees, you can achieve your dream.

Road commissioner: Try your best to save money for the government. Offer some attractive land price. But don't make Mr. Brown angry.

Possible outcome: win-win negotiation

Situation 6

MBA graduate: Emphasize your experiences and skills in negotiation and stick to your salary and position expectation, for it's the compensation for your MBA study.

Personnel director: Show him/her the prosperous future, comfortable working environments and relationships of your company. State that you can give him or her a good job title and better future pay although you cannot increase your salary offer by more than 5% now.

Possible outcome: win-win or win-lose negotiation

3. **Search for a negotiation case that reflects certain negotiation tactics—a case that impresses you most, then present your case to the class with analysis.**
4. **Discuss the following questions with your roommates after class. What exactly does bargaining mean? What does it involve? Why is bargaining so stressful? Does bargaining always involve an element of deception?**
5. **What is the key to successful bargaining? What is the most important word during the bargaining stage? How can you avoid misunderstandings during the bargaining stage?**

Job Interview

Unit Six

Objectives

To learn how to write a job application letter and a resume.
To learn some theme-related words, expressions and sentences in job interviews.
To learn useful etiquettes applied in job interviews.
To discuss and present ideas about job interviews.

Lead in

1. Have you ever written an application letter for further study, or a part-time job? Have you ever written your resume in English? What are the highlights?
2. Have you ever got a chance in an interview? If yes, state your experience for us. And what do you think you should prepare to succeed in an interview?

Text A

Introduction to Job Application Letter

A job application letter is a letter that accompanies your resume. It serves to introduce you to a prospective employer, makes a first impression about you and your writing ability, and prepares your prospective employer for what they will find in your resume. In other words, a job application letter is a highlight of your resume.

Features of Application Letters

1. Clearness. Focus on the subject—seeking a job, and don't beat about the bushes. The structure should also be clear so that the reader can easily get your point.

2. Conciseness. All the information included in the letter should be relevant to the job. Besides, use more short sentences than compound sentences.

3. Correctness. Be correct in your wording, and avoid too many spelling or punctuation mistakes.

4. Courtesy. Write in a proper tone. Show your respect to the receiver. But there is no need to flatter them. Self-respect is also very important.

Functions of Application Letters

A letter of application can be an important tool in helping you land an interview, or ultimately the job you seek. Although resumes and job applications highlight key skills, experience, and education, a letter of application serves other specific purposes as followed:

1. It can help you get the attention of potential employers. By taking the time to develop a letter of application, you can set yourself apart from those who don't.

2. It should also show off your writing and editing skills. In this sense, a letter of application is actually part of your writing portfolio and gives potential employers a sense of you.

3. As simple as it may sound, the letter of application is your primary tool for requesting an interview.

In conclusion, the job application letters you send explain to the employer why you are qualified for the position and why you should be selected for an interview. Use the letter to highlight relevant information from your resume, without duplicating it. Review how to decode a job ad so you know what the employer is looking for.

How to Write an Application Letter?

In a job application letter, it first tells the purpose of writing and introduces some brief background information about the applicant, mainly including name, age, nationality, education background, as well as work experience if there is any. All this needs to be mentioned only briefly. Finally leave your postal address, phone number, email address, and express thanks or the reader's attention to your letter. It may be sent by email. The following is the basic structure of an application letter.

Opening Paragraph: Who You Are and What You Want (Purpose)

    1. State the purpose of the letter and who you are.

    2. Name the position for which you are applying.

    3. State your personal interest in the company.

    4. Include how you heard of the position or the name of the person who referred you.

Paragraph Two: Why You Are a Good Candidate (Skills)

    Do not restate your resume. Use the cover letter to say things that you could not "fit" on your resume. Relate your skills and accomplishments to the employer's needs. Do not make the reader guess what you want and why you are qualified.

    1. Use specific examples to prove what you claim while remaining brief and to the point.

    2. Don't emphasize your desires. Focus on what you can contribute.

    3. Answer the question — "What can I do for the company?" Communicate in some special way that your skills can be valuable to the potential hirer.

Paragraph Three (Optional): Company Knowledge

    1. Use their language, jargon, and technology. Use the appropriate terms to indicate your ability and expertise.

    2. Tell them that you are familiar with the purposes and goals of the firm.

    3. Show how your personal philosophy about work, job, place, and profession fits with the purpose of the position.

    4. Use annual reports, recruiting brochures, and other company literature to obtain the information you

need to match your career goals with what the company has to offer.

Closing Paragraph: Next Step You Will Take

1. Keep it short and to the point.

2. State that your resume is enclosed for their review (this can be included in the first or second paragraphs also).

3. Include a specific request, such as for an interview or for a slot on their interview schedule.

4. Be clear about the next move and follow up: "I will phone you the week of September 1st to schedule a meeting."

5. Be assertive and take the initiative.

An ideal letter of application should cover one side of paper, and certainly no more than a side and a half. Such details as an easily legible font (Times New Roman, Arial) and laser printed version on high quality A4 paper are also essential.

Text B

How to Write a Resume?

Resume is a summary of an applicant's qualifications for employment or admission to college, usually in the form of an outline or list. In your resume, you should include all background information you think the reader should have about you and present the facts in the way that your reader will grasp them as quickly and efficiently as possible.

Developing a resume is the first step in any successful job search. The average resume is written out of necessity. Everyone knows you have to have one to get a job. Your resume is like your personal movie trailer. You want your resume to capture your employers' interest, so they'll want to learn more about you.

An effective resume will quickly highlight who you are, where you can be reached, and information about your most recent educational or training experiences. To make writing your resume as painless as possible, assemble the following information before you begin: personal information (such as name, address, phone, and e-mail address), current job, education and training, work experience (including duties and dates of employment), accomplishments (particularly as they relate to work experience), specific skills and abilities, as well as information about software knowledge or machinery you can operate.

Writing a resume applies some strict rules. It should be clear and concise, 1—2 pages should be the maximum. Be honest about your experience and goals (but present them in the best possible light). Stress what you can do and what you've learned. Be neat no typos, smudges, etc.. Don't forget to include volunteer work, work and school awards and honors, notable skills that your employers are interested in. Make the most of your experience. Be proud of what you've done in the past. This helps make a positive impression.

Main contents of a resume typically consists of personal information, job objective, qualifications, work experience, educational background, technical qualifications, publications and patents, social activities, honors & awards, references, conclusion/ summary/ personal statement.

Personal information: Includes your name, address, email, and telephone number.

Sample:

> (Address until July 10, 2010)
> 112 Guilin Road, Apt. 401 Shanghai, 200034
> Email: lxm@yahoo.com
> 021-85557221
> Li Xinmin

Objective: Briefly states the job (or type of work) you are applying for.

Summary of achievements (optional): Emphasizes your major achievements.

Qualifications: Your education and work experience.

Education: Includes degrees and dates, fields of study and institutions, as well as any scholarships, educational awards and academic honors if you have excelled academically.

Work Experience: Includes all your work experience related to your job objectives, with job titles, dates of employment, places, firms, duties and responsibilities.

Compare the following two ways of writing:

1. 1998—2002   Office Manager for Carson's, Inc., Chicago.

2. 1998—2002   Office Manager for Carson's, Inc., Chicago. Supervised a staff of seven in processing company records and communications.

References: Includes accurate mailing address, with appropriate job titles if you provide any.

Sample Reference:

> Dr. Jin Daming, Professor of Finance
> Bejing University
> Bejing, 100079
> 010-85981234

There are two types of resumes: the chronological resume and the functional resume. Chronological resume is also called the reverse resume for it lists the jobs you've had going backward in time, from the current one to your first. Functional resume lists the applicant's main capabilities and competence.

To lessen the chance of your resume being directed toward the wastebasket or deleted with a click of the mouse, you should be mindful of the following four points. Your resume should be brief and easy to read. It should be to-the-point, attractive and be error-free. Last but not the least, you should always tell the truth.

Case Study

Case One: (Indented style application letter)

Dear Sir /Madam,

I am writing with the hope that you might have a position for an English major student. In order to get started in this career, I am willing to accept any position where I can demonstrate my competence and move upward according to my abilities with leadership, quantitative, analytical and communication skills.

I am a self-confident, diligent and decisive young woman with good command of English listening, speaking and writing. Meanwhile, I am a frequent user of computer.

My ability to work well as part of the team, combined with my enthusiasm to learn, were essential to my contributions and success during my four years study. I believe that I can apply the same skills to a position within your company.

I look forward to discussing the position with you in more details. I will call next week to see if you agree that my qualifications seem to be a match for the position. If so, I hope to schedule an interview at a mutually convenient time. Thank you for your consideration.

Yours sincerely,
Rita

Case Two: (Full block style application letter)

Dear Sir or Madam,

I learned from *Beijing Youth Daily* Jan.2 that your company is offering a position for a secretary, and it's a great pleasure for me to write to explore the possibility of seeking the job.

I graduated two years ago from Nanjing University, and obtained a bachelor's degree in the field of business management. During my stay in the university my major courses included macro-economics, business communication skills, marketing and computer applications. I was especially fond of the communication skills which enabled me to deal with people and thing around well.

Upon graduation I engaged with HP China Branch as an assistant to the head of Marketing Department. My responsibilities consisted of carrying out market surveys, writing reports and organizing meetings within the department. This two-year experience has helped me a lot in many ways. In particular, I become increasingly aware of the importance of co-ordination and co-operation among co-workers. I also believe the experience will qualify me for the current vacancy in your company.

I passed CET-6 with high marks. My spoken English is also fluent enough to organize meetings in English, which was actually my routine work in HP. Most of my market reports were presented in English, as my former boss is a native English speaker.

I enclose herein my resume and some relevant documents as required. And if you need any further information on me, I also refer you to Mr. Johnson, my ex-colleague, who is available at 021-66668888.

I appreciate your sincere consideration of me, and am looking forward to an early interview with you.

Sincerely yours,

Wang Peng

Case Three: (Resume)

Personal Information:

Family Name: Wang	Given Name: Bin
Date of Birth: July 12, 1989	Birth Place: Beijing
Sex: Male	Marital Status: Unmarried
Telephone: (010)62771234	E-mail:carrieera@163.com

Objective:

To obtain a challenging position as a software engineer with an emphasis in software design and development.

Educational Background:

1997.9—2000.6 Dept. of Automation, Graduate School of Tsinghua University, M.E.

1993.9—1997.7 Dept. of Automation, Beijing Institute of Technology, B.E.

Main Courses:

Mathematics

Advanced Mathematics, Probability and Statistics, Linear Algebra

Engineering Mathematics, Numerical Algorithm, Operational Algorithm

Functional Analysis Linear and Nonlinear Programming

Electronics and Computer

Circuit Principal Data Structures, Digital Electronics

Artificial Intelligence Computer, Local Area Network

Computer Abilities:

Skilled in use of MS FrontPage, Win 95/NT, Sun, JavaBeans, HTML, CGI, JavaScript, Perl, Visual Interdev, Distributed Objects, CORBA, C, C++, Project 98, Office 97, Rational Requisite Pro, Process, Pascal, PL/I and SQL software

English Skills:

Have a good command of both spoken and written English. Past CET-6, TOEFL:

623; GRE: 2213

Scholarships and Awards

    1999.3 Guanghua First-class Scholarship for graduate

    1998.11 Metal Machining Practice Award

    1997.4 Academic Progress Award

Qualifications:

    General business knowledge relating to financial, healthcare

    Have a passion for the Internet, and an abundance of common sense. Be able to work under a dynamic environment. Have coordination skills, teamwork spirit. Studious nature and dedication are my greatest strengths.

Reference:

    Available upon request.

Case Four: (Resume)

    Lin Jian

    125 Zhongshan Road

    Nanjing, Jiangsu 210023

    Email: linjian@yahoo.com

    025-4418390

    Job Objective: Manager in marketing research

    Education: Sept.2010—July 2014 Bachelor of Business Administration, Najing University

    Major: Marketing

    Minor: General Business; Marketing Courses; Marketing Principle; Advertising Media; Marketing Research; Marketing Management

    Other Business Courses: Business Statistics; Business Finance; Business Communication; Business Law

    Grades: 90 average in all marketing courses. Made 5s on all research reports; two were exhibited as models of excellence.

    Work Experience:

    July—August, 2010 Sales person, Lixing Cutting-ware Company. Made special deliveries, assisted customers, did stock keeping.

June—September, 2011 Sales representative, Bigman Publishing House. Sold books door to door.

Organizations:

Jianxiong Debating Club, 2011—2012;

Managing Editor of Horizon (student poetry magazine), 2010—2012;

Tennis team, 2011—2012.

Hobbies: tennis, writing short stories.

Personal data:

Reference

Notes

1. **Letter of Application Checklist**

    1) Does the letter have a clear introduction, body, and conclusion?

    2) Does the letter contain information that's relevant to the position you seek?

    3) Does the introduction include a forecasting statement, and does the body follow through with the topics and organization forecasted?

    4) Does the letter supplement, not merely repeat, the information contained in the resume or job application form?

    5) Does the letter provide specific examples—numbers, excerpts, comments, or scenarios—that back up your statements of competency?

    6) Does the letter focus on how your skills/education/experience/knowledge can benefit the company?

    7) Does the letter use block or modified-block style correctly?

    8) Is the letter limited to one page (or does it appropriately provide information specifically requested)?

    9) Does the letter include contact information? Is the letter signed?

    10) Does the letter look clean, and is it free from errors (no typos, no grammar/punctuation errors, and no formatting errors)?

2. **Notes on writing application letter**

   Dos:

   1) Include the person's full name, title, company name, and company address.

   2) Include your full name, address, and contact information.

   3) Use a formal greeting, such as Mr., Ms., Dr..

   4) Mention how you found out about the position.

   5) Be upbeat and creative—make your letter stand out.

   6) Keep copies of everything you send.

   Don'ts:

   1) Don't write a long letter. Shorter is better.

   2) Don't address the person by first name unless you know him or her personally and have permission to do so.

   3) Don't forget to personally sign the letter.

   4) Don't forget to check grammar and spelling.

   5) Don't use flashy stationery (unless you're applying for a highly creative job).

   6) Don't use slang.

3. **Typical beginnings and endings in an application letter**

   1) I wish to apply for the position advertised in the newspaper.

   2) I have heard that perhaps you might need an executive secretary with considerable experience working experience.

   3) I would like to apply for the position of secretary which you advertised in the newspaper of June 15.

   4) I would like to inquire about the position of business manager that you advertised in the newspaper in September 5.

   5) I have learned that you are looking for an engineer has had some general experience in business and I desire to apply for the position.

   6) Your organization is more than just a business house. It is an institution in the minds of the local public. It has a reputation for fair play and honesty with both employees and customers alike.

   7) For the past four years, while specializing in international trade at college, I have had a secret ambition to work for your organization. I will graduate in July this year.

8) In response to your advertisement in today's newspaper, I wish to apply for the position of senior clerk in your esteemed firm.
9) I am enclosing my qualifications which prompt me to make application now.
10) I have enclosed a resume as well as a brief sample of my writing for your review. I look forward to meeting with you to discuss further how I could contribute to your organization.

Useful Words and Expressions

1. Personal information
   - native place 籍贯
   - province 省/city 市/ county 县
   - autonomous region 自治区
   - prefecture 专区
   - nationality 民族，国籍
   - citizenship 国籍
   - marital status 婚姻状况
   - married 已婚/ single /unmarried 未婚/ divorced 离异
   - ID card number 身份证号码
   - date of availability 可到职时间

2. Educational background
   - bachelor 学士
   - post doctorate 博士后
   - doctor (Ph.D) 博士
   - master 硕士
   - abroad student 留学生
   - graduate student 研究生
   - undergraduate 大学肄业生
   - major 主修
   - minor 副修
   - educational highlights 课程重点部分
   - specialized courses 专门课程
   - courses taken 所学课程

3. Work experience and other expressions
   - social practice 社会实践
   - summer / vacation jobs 暑期/假期工作
   - extracurricular 课外活动
   - academic activities 学术活动
   - special training 特别训练
   - off-job training 脱产培训
   - in-job training 在职培训
   - government-supported 公费生
   - commoner 自费生
   - intern 实习生

adaptable 适应性强的	aggressive 有进取心的
	ambitious 有雄心壮志的
amiable 和蔼可亲的	amicable 友好的
	analytical 善于分析的
initiative 首创精神	inventive 创造力的
	knowledgeable 有见识的
kind-hearted 好心的	loyal 忠心耿耿的
	open-minded 虚心的
painstaking 辛勤的	persevering 不屈不挠的
	strong-willed 意志坚强的
listic 实事求是的	reliable 可信赖的
	self-conscious 自觉的

4. Career/job objective

position desired 希望职位　　　position applied for / sought 申请职位

for prospects of promotion 为晋升的前途

for wider experience 为扩大工作经验

due to expiry of employment 由于雇用期满

to look for a more challenging opportunity 找一个更有挑战性的工作机会

Supplementary Materials

Job Etiquette

Job etiquette refers to good manners and proper behavior that are essential for our professional growth.

In the world of competition, it is very difficult to get a job and hence getting one could be quite an achievement. To survive and sustain for long in our professional field, we should maintain some rules that have social values. The words "job etiquette" refer to polite, warm and friendly behavior of an individual that he/she should maintain at the workplace. As a social being, we need to cultivate some moral and social values, such as discipline, punctuality and friendliness.

Importance of Etiquette at the Workplace

Recruiters are always in search of candidates with strong interpersonal skills and etiquette. In the world of a challenging job market, it is really very difficult to succeed. We should be very meticulous about our behavior. A small wrongdoing can create a negative impression of us. However, once you get through the job interview and follow proper job etiquette, you can make further progress by winning approval of your colleagues and thus working for your promotion in the office. Proper etiquette helps in winning the hearts of recruiters as well as the senior managers, apart from your

colleagues.

Forms of Job Etiquette

Job etiquette or office etiquette refers to conversation etiquette, greeting etiquette, communication etiquette, dress etiquette, dealing with clients, good manners, etc. Dress etiquette differs according to the job profile. For example, the dress code in IT companies can differ from that in a publishing house. Here's a look at some tips to maintain proper job etiquette. These tips will definitely prove helpful in your career growth.

1. Conversation Etiquette

While conversing with your colleague or other people, always look into his/her eyes. Instead of getting into irrelevant topics and discussion, make your conversation short and brief.

2. Listen and Try to be Attentive

From the very first day, try to be attentive and listen carefully to what others say. Listening attentively is a form of art, through which you can win the heart of your seniors and colleagues. Your attentiveness and careful listening can help you learn things quickly. Hence, you can succeed in your career.

3. Greeting Etiquette

When you are getting introduced to other people, shake hands. Make sure that your handshake is short and firm and that it conveys confidence. If you are being introduced, then stand up and greet the individual.

4. Effective Communication Etiquette

Effective workplace communication etiquette refers to using communication routes efficiently, via e-mail and phone. An important phone etiquette is to lower the volume of the cell phone or phone call, while taking a call, so that it does not offend your boss or colleagues.

On the other hand, while communicating with your co-worker through e-mails, always address the person with hi/hello or dear, followed by a title and ending with "Yours sincerely" or "Yours truly." It is better to use friendly, yet formal language.

5. Do Not Take Things for Granted

From the very beginning, try to be alert and don't take things for granted. Don't show your laziness by depending on others. Rather, show eagerness to shoulder your responsibilities.

6. Work Sincerely

To be sincere and hardworking in your work is very important. You should not take any short cuts to finish your work or duty.

7. Managing Deadlines

You should try to complete your work within the time schedule and deliver it according to the target fixed by your boss. Sometimes, if it is not possible to finish your work during office hours, then you can take the work home and try to finish it.

8. Proper Dressing Sense

Proper dress code is another essential element of job etiquette. You should wear neat and clean clothes, in which you feel comfortable and look good. Here, personal cleanliness and professional dress code play a vital role.

9. Proper Table Manners

Once you enter your office, you need to be formal in every way. At the office lunch table, follow proper table manners that include not talking when your mouth is full, not to make noise while eating, proper handling of fork and spoon, not to cough while eating, etc. These table manners help a person in being more civilized and respectable at the workplace.

10. Respect the Rules

Workplace has its set of rules and regulations. A good employee always shows respect for those rules; this helps him/her to remain committed and devoted to his/her job.

11. Friendly Attitude

Friendly attitude is another element of job etiquette. Try to be relaxed, happy and friendly and share a good rapport with everyone around you. For this, you need to be confident and have belief in yourself. Always remember that a jolly face wins a thousand hearts.

12. Avoid Office Politics

Avoiding office politics is another thing that one needs to put an effort into. Always pay regards to your colleagues and stay away from all kinds of backbiting and gossiping. Avoid belittling or offending your co-workers or any former employers.

13. Do Not Interrupt

Refrain from disturbing or interrupting your colleagues while they are busy with their work. Try to maintain a peaceful and calm atmosphere around you.

14. Adjust Yourself According to the Environment

You should be able to adjust yourself according to the environment. For this, you should have some information about the dress code and rules of work at your office and try to adjust with the environment as well as colleagues.

Tips on Following Job Etiquette

Apart from the above mentioned etiquette, there are some other codes of behavior that one should maintain in the office premise. These are:

1. Try to reach your workplace on time.
2. Be enthusiastic.
3. Do not argue.
4. Be helpful to your colleagues.
5. Maintain your personal cleanliness.
6. Cultivate a positive attitude towards others.
7. Do not be partial.

Thus, job etiquette refers to civilized behavior that should be maintained at the workplace. Always remember "love begets love." If you expect good behavior from others, then first you have to behave in a proper way. Keeping this in mind, if you follow the etiquette mentioned above, then you are definitely one step closer towards success.

Questions:

1. *Besides what has been mentioned in the passage, can you list any other forms of job etiquettes?*
2. *Apparently, nowadays cubicle has become the standard business configuration, even for managers. What are the rules for cubicle etiquette in your mind?*
3. *Make a comparison between western and Chinese table manners and present it to the class.*

Assignments

1. Translate the following letter into English.

亲爱的李先生：

我在今晚的地方报纸上看到了你们的招聘广告，我想在这个夏天做一份服务生的工作，敬请考虑。

我十七岁，现在正在学习英文和经济学。毕业后，我希望能够学习酒店管理课程。去年暑假时，我在中央酒店作服务生，在此期间，我的工作能力和态度受到了周围同事的赞赏和好评。

如果您能寄给我有关这份工作的薪水和工作环境的一些信息，我会非常高兴。

期待着您的回音，谢谢！

李明

2. Write an application letter according to the following advertisement.

IBM (International Business Machines Corporation) is now looking for fresh graduates to join our company as technical writers.

Job requirements

• Major in computer science, electronic engineering, English, or equivalent.

• Excellent in English written and oral communication (please specify the details of your English skills in the resume, e.g. the scores of CET-6, TEM-8, TOFEL, IELTS, or GRE).

• Must be detail-oriented and commit to deadlines.

• Good teamwork spirit and fast learning capabilities.

• Interested in computer technologies and familiar with its concepts.

• Candidate with related work experiences is preferred, graduate student with good technical understanding and good English is preferred.

3. Make a short conversation of about 200 words according to the following situation. Role-play the conversation in pais.

Zhang Xiaodong, a senior student majoring in international trade, is going to graduate from a university. He has an interview with Mr. Henry Hudson.

Useful Expressions

• provide me with a good opportunity to use my knowledge

• Permanent Normal Trade Relation

• tariff preference for imported goods

• fringe benefits

- attend the training program
- do my utmost
- notify you of our decision

4. Work in pairs. Suppose you are an interviewer, and your partner is applying for a job of office clerk. Form a dialogue by using the useful sentences and expressions you've learned in this unit.

Office Clerk Wanted by Xinhua Electronic Company

Requirements: college graduate, familiar with Microsoft Office 2010, fluent in English, strong flexibility and independence, at least one year of related experience, overtime work preferred.

---

5. Write an application letter according to the following advertisement.

P&G is now looking for Year 2014 fresh graduates to join our company as HR trainees. We believe that we are in a very good position to offer you a variety of career options across our Business Units and Functions.

Position: HR trainee

Requirements:
- Outgoing personality and teamwork spirit
- Customer-friendly attitude and good communication skills
- Quick learner and excellent execution skills
- Superior written & oral English is a plus
- Microsoft Office talent is a plus